ABOUT THE AUTHOR

Gordon Cheers has been growing Carnivorous Plants for eight years, and in the last four, while travelling Australia and overseas to see Carnivorous Plants, has managed a wholesale Carnivorous Plant nursery. This has given him the opportunity to meet not only Botanists and commercial growers, but also Carnivorous Plant enthusiasts. It is with this knowledge gained over the years that Gordon has written this book to dispel many of the myths of Carnivorous Plants, and given practical advice on how to grow these most interesting plants.

Lower pitcher of Nepenthes Rokko. An attractive hybrid of Nepenthes Thorelii with its narrow rim, red short and fat pitchers and Maxima with its patchy burgundy colouration, predominant wide rim and long thin pitchers. ▲

Carnivorous Plants

By Gordon Cheers

Dedicated to my parents with love

Published by
Carnivor and Insectivor Plants
PO Box 78
Diamond Creek
Victoria, 3089
Australia

Printed by Globe Press, Melbourne
1983

Design, lay-out, typesetting by
Correct Line Graphics
Melbourne
Correct Line Graphics is a worker
Co-operative assisted by the Victorian
Co-operative Development Program

Photographs by
Larry Pitt: cover, pages 19 (large),
21, 27, 29, 32, 33, 35, 36, 40, 41,
44, 47, 48, 59, 68, 70, 75, back cover.
Alan Jager: pages 2, 19 (inset), 30,
31, 39, 51, 52, 57, 58, 60, 63,
72, 73, 79, 82, 86, 88, 91.

ISBN 0–9591937–0–7

© All rights reserved. No part of this publication may be reproduced, stored in a retrieval system or transmitted by any form or by any means, electronic, mechanical, photocopying, recording or otherwise, without the prior permission of the publisher.

Contents

About the Author		1
Dedication		4
Acknowledgements		6
Introduction		9
Chapter 1	Past History	11
Chapter 2	How To Choose Carnivorous Plants That Will Thrive For You	13
Chapter 3	Venus Fly Trap	17
Chapter 4	Pitcher Plants	23
Chapter 5	Albany Pitcher Plant	38
Chapter 6	Sun Pitchers	43
Chapter 7	Sundews	46
Chapter 8	Hanging Pitcher Plants	54
Chapter 9	Butterworts	67
Chapter 10	Bladderworts	71
Chapter 11	Cobra Lily	77
Chapter 12	Rainbow Plants	81
Chapter 13	Summer Growth and Winter Dormancy	83
Chapter 14	Peat Gardens and Terraria	86
Equipment Required		93
References		95

ACKNOWLEDGEMENTS

It isn't possible to write a book on Carnivorous Plants without having to rely on many individuals, whether the help is in terms of layout, photography, drawings, editing or just from growers who gave advice on how they have grown their plants. While it isn't possible to name everybody, the names mentioned come close to thanking some of the people who contributed. They include Alan Jager and Larry Pitt for their photographs; Alice Mills for her help with the editing; Patricia Pollard for the drawings; Stefanie Hamel for the typing; also Sonny Pereira, without whom the Nepenthes section would be incomplete.

MAP DESCRIPTION

The world maps have been included as a guide to where the different species of Carnivorous Plants are native, and also to give an idea of how widespread a particular genus is. These maps are designed to help give some indication as to the climate the plants are native to. However it should be mentioned that factors such as altitude and closeness to sea breezes, etc. can have quite a dramatic effect on climate.

Many species are native to more than one area. When this occurs an attempt has been made to determine the area in which the plant was first discovered, and only this single area has been marked on the map.

8

Introduction

This book was written to answer some of the questions that both beginners in the field of Carnivorous Plants and Carnivorous Plant collectors have asked over the eight years I have been growing these plants.

Many books have been written on Carnivorous Plants, detailing leaf structure, type of flowers, etc.; however few books give information on how to grow these plants.

Most of the information on growing requirements I mention in this book has been gained through trial and error, from my own experiences, and from growers I have known. As far as possible I have given general growing requirements, but as the plants will be grown in vastly different areas, with varying degrees of temperature, humidity and sunlight, this book should only be used as a guide. Often one grower may grow plants in full sun, water from a tray and use fertilizers, while another will use a misting system, filtered sunlight and never fertilize; yet both will have plants that look equally good, and each will swear by their particular method, vowing "mine is the best".

What is important in growing these plants is to know what to look for in a sick plant, and what to do (or not to do) to the plant when this sickness is noticed.

As a general principle, a sick plant should never be fertilized, fed meat, etc. In fact I never feed my plants meat, flies, ants and so on; the plants catch enough insects on their own to be healthy, and force feeding can kill the plants, especially is they are not grown in the right conditions.

Dispelling the myths which declare that Carnivorous Plants need to be fed regularly, that they are difficult to grow, and that there are plants that can eat people, is the intention of this book.

I hope this book will clear up some hitherto unanswered questions for you, about what I consider the most interesting plants known to man.

Gordon Cheers.

Past History 1

*M*uch has been said about plants that can eat animals. An article written in 1900 described and gave dramatic illustrations of plants such as the Bladderwort swallowing a crocodile, and an enormous Venus Fly Trap springing shut on its unfortunate human victim. The writer goes on to say "that in years to come Carnivorous Plants may become a real threat to animals and people" although this may take many years to evolve. Shades of John Wyndham's "Day of the Triffids"!

The truth is not quite so dramatic. At the present time no man-eating plants are known to exist. But there are plants around that are truly carnivorous, (flesh-eating), which have as their prey insects, small birds and even small monkeys. These plants use a variety of traps to capture their food. They include traps which when touched snap shut after sucking victims in, and send out a sticky substance which makes escape as difficult as climbing out of a honey jar; plants that have a pit fall which at its base has a digestive liquid which dissolves prey away; or plants with an inner structure like a mirror maze with a hidden door. It is the structure of these traps as well as the care of the plants that this book is designed to elaborate on.

Over the last few years the fascination and beauty of Carnivorous Plants has been described by many people. It is sometimes thought that this is a new discovery, but the insect-eaters were very popular last century as well. In fact in Victorian times a glass-house was not considered complete unless it had large dangling Carnivorous Plants (a Nepenthes) hanging from the rafters. So after a century of neglect we are now rediscovering this fascinating form of plant. Botanists have never lost sight of the Carnivores, and a great deal of study has been carried out on their trapping mechanism and growing habitat. All this information can be used, as we will see in the remainder of this book, to help us find the best way of growing these plants in our gardens and hot-houses, and to encourage them to their most spectacular form.

One botanist of the last century, J.D. Hooker, a colleague of Darwin's, writes: "the digestion of the plant is like that of animals...it has a nervous system" and he comes very close to suggesting that Carnivorous Plants are the link between animals and plants. Others have speculated that a carnivorous diet is on the increase in plants. Perhaps growing and studying Carnivorous Plants we are watching evolution in action.

In the past many plants that in some way caught an animal or insect were considered carnivorous. Such a plant is the Roridula from South Africa, commonly called the Fly Paper Plant. This plant only holds flies or insects, like fly paper, but has no ability (glands) to aid digestion, and hence is unable to absorb the insects' nutrients. This isn't to say a plant needs to be active to be carnivorous; it can be passive and still fall into the carnivorous plant family.

Passive carnivorous plants are those like the Cephalotus which require the insect to move towards the plant, then fall down into a pit of digestive liquid. This pit secretes enzymes similar to those humans have in their stomachs, and this gives the plant the ability to absorb nourishment from the insect.

Active plants can be defined as those that catch the insect, hold it and eventually dissolve it away. The most well known of this group is the Venus Fly Trap. There are plants that don't exactly fall into either category. These are the Pinguiculas. The Pinguiculas can be considered semi-active in that the plant releases a sticky substance upon being touched by an insect. There has also been much confusion about trigger plants which while active in that they respond to the presence of insects or humans, are not carnivorous because their springing action simply sprays pollen over the insect to aid fertilization.

2

How to Choose Carnivorous Plants that will Thrive for You

Different Carnivorous Plants can be grown in a very wide variety of conditions. Some will live happily in peat gardens, outside, with no special protection. Others need glass houses or shade houses. Some will grow inside houses on kitchen shelves or in terraria. A few need very special growing conditions, watering systems and constant high temperatures. It is important to be aware of the needs of the Carnivorous Plants you buy and not expect them to do well all together in the same environment.

The growing conditions in which Carnivorous plants do well fall into three main categories:

(A) Some grow in the wild in swamps or bogs in areas like North America. These are hardy enough to be grown outdoors, if your temperatures are between -5 degrees C. (23 F.) and 15 degrees C. (60 F.) in winter and 10 degrees C. (50 F.) and 35 degrees C. (95 F.) in summer;

(B) Those that grow in tropical jungle canopies, coming from areas such as Malaysia and New Guinea, and usually should be grown in hothouses; and

(C) Those that like a cool root system and a fairly even temperature because they are native to high mountain areas such as North America (Mt. Shaston), South America (Mt. Roraima) and Borneo (Mt. Kinabalu). This latter group of plants need special conditions to keep the plant healthy and should only be attempted by the experienced grower. The Venus Fly Trap (*Dionaea Muscipula*) falls into group (A), as do most of the *Sarracenias* (Pitcher plants) and the West Australian Pitcher Plant (*Cephalotus Follicularis*).

Group (A)

SWAMP PLANTS

Dionaea (Venus Fly Trap) is the best known of all Carnivorous Plants, because of its dramatic trap mechanism. But the fascination of trying out the trap mechanism has led to proud plant owners actually killing the plants.

I have found that a lot of growers have their Dionaea die on them because they either spring all the traps regularly or feed the plant chicken, meat, etc., or flies sprayed with insecticide. While many people do feed their plants regularly, I feel it can cause more harm than good. The plants catch enough food for themselves.

As the Dionaea grows naturally in peat bogs this means that it requires moist soil all year round. This also means that if the plant is watered with tap water there is a chance that salts will build up and eventually cause the plant to die.

Sarracenias (tall Pitcher Plants) are the largest of all the Carnivorous Plants. Sarracenias have tube-like pitchers that grow to three feet; they are passive carnivores, and have downward pointing hairs that make access easy for an insect and departure impossible. Just inside the lip the plant has a nectar zone which together with the plant colour attracts insects down the tube. Towards the base of the pitcher, glands secrete a digestive enzyme which like the dionaea dissolves the insect and provides the plant with nourishment. Altogether there are eight species of Sarracenia and they include *Alata, Flava, Purpurea, Psittacina, Minor, Rubra, Leucophylla* and *Oreophylla*.

One of the characteristics that makes Sarracenia popular is that they have large flowers appearing in spring, often rising above the pitchers on slender stalks. These can be cross pollinated easily and new hybrids developed. Sarracenias and Sundews can be planted outside in peat gardens which can be made to look like natural swamps or bogs.

Sundews (*Drosera*) usually require filtered light and when the conditions are right have droplets of water on the tips of the leaves. These droplets appear on tentacles and contain a sticky substance which holds the insect to the plant, and a digestive enzyme which in time dissolves most bugs away. Mature plants of the *Pygmaea Drosera* could fit on a five cent coin (one cm) and plants like *Drosera Peltata* grow up to 30cm high (12 inches). With many Drosera an insect landing on one tentacle causes other tentacles to move towards the insect and eventually engulf it. In time all that is left of the bug is hard shell to be blown away by the wind.

Drosera are among the easiest plants to look after. The droplets indicate that the plant is surviving quite well. If the droplets disappear than covering the plant with a plastic bag helps them redevelop till the plant can be moved to a more appropriate position. The same can be done with the West Australian Pitcher Plant (*Cephalotus Follicularis*) except in this case it's the lid that closes as the humidity drops.

Cephalotus Follicularis has little shoe-like pitchers with a lid, which during rain storms closes and stops the pitcher from getting flooded, and during dry spells closes and stops the pitcher from drying out. In full sun the plant turns a dark burgundy colour almost approaching black. Insects become attracted to the nectar zones just inside the rim and fall into the pitcher.

Group (B)

TROPICAL PLANTS

While most Sarracenia, Drosera and Cephalotus like quite cold conditions, the *Nepenthes* would die, as these plants come from rain forests.

Tropical plants such as Nepenthes have long pitchers hanging from the tips of the leaves. It is these plants that have been responsible for many of the myths of Carnivorous Plants. Some of the pitchers measure up to 20cm (8 inches) and have been known to entrap birds and small monkeys. Because most Nepenthes are grown in the tropics, except for Nepenthes Khasiana, they require a temperature range of between 15 and 30 degrees C. (60 to 85 degrees F.) Ideally to grow these plants they also need a relative humidity of at least 70%. If the heat is increased without an increase in humidity the plant may grow quite well but won't form pitchers. If the humidity drops too low and the atmosphere becomes dry, the lid will begin to wither and eventually the whole pitcher will wither and die.

Nepenthes can be grown inside the house provided they are kept in terraria. For increased care soil heaters and artificial lighting can also be added.

Group (C)

HIGH ALTITUDE PLANTS

Sun Pitchers (*Heliamphora*) look like the new leaves on an aspidistra and fall into category (C) of growing conditions. They grow as natives only in Venezuala on high plateaus, which due to their inaccessibility have isolated the area from the rest of the world in terms of both plants and animals. Many people believe that due to their isolation the Heliamphora provide the link between "normal" plants and the carnivorous Sarracenia. The spectacular Cobra Lily (*Darlingtonia Californica*) is native to North America and like the Heliamphora grows at high altitudes and likes a cool root system.

Darlingtonia is often covered with snow in winter, which melts to provide a cool root system in summer. It is commonly called Cobra Lily, as it looks like a snake with fangs about to strike. In fact this plant is another of the pitcher plants, that is, the plant is passive with downward pointing hairs.

LITTLE KNOWN CARNIVOROUS PLANTS

There is a small group of Carnivorous Plants that are quite rare in cultivation for various reasons. For example the Drosophyllum Lusitanicum has only one species existing; the Fungas Arthrobotrys Obligiospora is so small that a microscope is needed to view it; both the Aldrovanda Vesiculosa and the Genlisea float on water as well as being extremely difficult to see with the naked eye.

As the above species are so difficult to obtain and even more difficult to cultivate, I have had limited experience in growing them myself. I suggest readers who are interested in growing these rare plants obtain some of the references mentioned at the end of this book for more detailed information.

3

Venus Fly Traps (Dionaea Muscipula)

Venus Fly Trap is the most well known of all the Carnivorous Plants. It is usually the first Carnivorous Plant that budding growers purchase, and I believe it is the plant that inspired the mythology of the plants that can trap people. Charles Darwin, in his book "Insectivorous Plants" said of the Venus Fly Trap that it is the "most wonderful plant in the world".

For many people the *Dionaea* is the most interesting plant because it is active, that is it responds with a trapping mechanism towards its prey. I hope by the time you finish this book you will feel that other Carnivorous Plants, though less spectacular in action, are equally fascinating to grow or observe.

Distribution of Dionaea Muscipula ▼

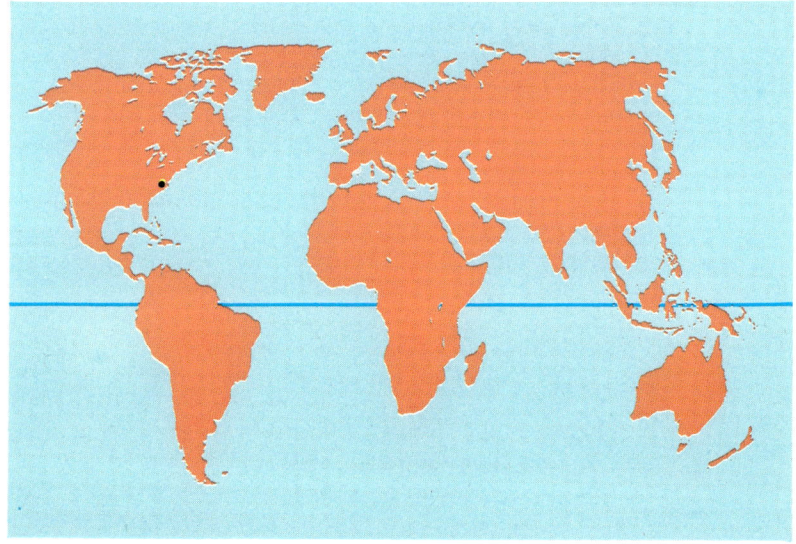

A common misbelief is that if you put your finger in the trap of a Venus Fly Trap, you will lose it, or at least it will get bitten. This is not the case; all that will happen is that the trap will close around your finger, and it is very easy to pull away. The plant uses energy in both opening and closing the trap, and this energy, which is actually a growth in the walls of the trap, is gained from absorbing the minerals from insects it has caught. Therefore, if the traps are continuously sprung by fingers, sticks and the like, the trap will eventually die. If this is done often enough to all of the traps, the whole plant will die.

You may find that feeding dead flies and ants to your plants will cause the traps to go black and die off. This is due to the fact that a live insect will struggle in a closed trap, causing the trigger hairs just inside the trap to be stimulated into closing the trap tighter and tighter. When the trap is totally sealed an enzyme enters, and in time dissolves the soft parts of the insect. This may take days or perhaps weeks, depending on the size of the insect, the size of the trap, and the growing conditions.

If the area where the plant is growing is very dry and hot then the trap may close slowly, or not at all, and may or may not dissolve the insect. Undissolved meat soon rots, and subsequently the trap will rot. Feeding dead flies to your plant simulates these conditions, and the plant may simply not be able to digest the food you offer and so rot along with it.

After catching and dissolving an insect, the trap will eventually open, in approximately ten days, exposing only the outer shell, legs and hard parts of the body of the dead insect. This is then blown away by the wind and the trap is left ready for another feed.

Three insects is usually the maximum any trap will catch. The trap has then outlived its usefulness and will die, to be replaced by a bigger trap, although this too depends on the age of the plant and the conditions it is grown in.

Most Venus Fly Traps have six traps on each bulb. If you see a plant that has twelve leaves or more, then you are looking at two plants, as the bulb of the original plant has divided into two. In this case, the plant can be divided and potted up into separate pots.

Apart from bulb division as a method of propogation of Venus Fly Trap, this plant can also be grown by seed.

Flowers appear in spring, and they have small white petals, as can be seen from the photo opposite. There is usually anything from 3–15 flowers on a stem, which often rises to 30cm (12 inches high).

Dionaea Muscipula

To obtain viable seeds the easiest method is to get flowers from two different plants and brush one against the other. Then in a couple of months these flowers will die, producing a black seed pod, containing small black seeds.

The seeds should be sprinkled onto a tray of damp peat moss, then well watered. After having sprayed the tray with a fungicide, it should be covered with a plastic bag. Seedlings should appear in about four weeks. When they have achieved a size of 19mm (¾ inch) across they can be potted up.

Fly Traps usually grow in one of two ways: either with tall and skinny leaves raised into the air, or with short, fat leaves close to the soil. This latter type has bigger and redder traps. Both these types of the Venus Fly Trap can be equally healthy and catch many insects. To a large extent the former type can be achieved by increasing humidity, keeping the soil drier and restricting the sunlight. This of course means that a plant grown with lower humidity, damper soil and a high amount of sunlight will have shorter and redder traps.

CARE

If your plant is growing in such a way that it has long leaves with tiny traps which go black and die, then it is highly likely the plant is not getting enough sunlight. As a guide your Fly Trap requires

Venus Fly Trap from seeds grown in a tray

Inset: Flower of Venus Fly Trap ▼

at least four hours sunlight during summer. The plant can be grown outside in full sunlight quite successfully, if it is kept moist and the temperature doesn't go above 35 degrees C. (95 degrees F.) for any great length of time. Under these conditions the inside of the traps should begin to turn red as summer approaches. If the plant is kept in a pot it should be sitting in ten to twenty mm of water, (half to one inch), depending on the size of the pot. The pot should not be allowed to dry out over this summer period. If this does happen then gradually increase the amount of water, and if the bulb is large enough the plant will grow back to its original size.

If the tall leaves begin to droop downwards this is usually an indication that the humidity is too low; that is, the atmosphere is too dry. When this happens cover the pot with a plastic bag, or a glass dome of some sort, and reduce the sunlight. In a very short time the leaves will pick up again and return to their original position.

Black leaves and traps should be cut off and removed from the growing area; this will prevent grey mould from appearing. This mould or fungus can affect healthy plants, as the airborne spores can travel from dead or dying leaves to healthy plants. A spray with a fungicide (such as BENLATE) could be used to prevent this occurring.

Venus Fly Traps are native to North Carolina in the USA. This area has an average winter temperature of 10 degrees C. (50 degrees F.). If the plant isn't allowed to go through a winter dormancy period then it may be weaker during summer. If the plant is deprived of its dormancy period year after year it will eventually die.

One very easy way to look after your plant during winter is to cut off all its leaves and traps and place the bulb (free of soil) in the refrigerator during the winter period. Then as spring approaches spray the bulb with Benlate before potting up. When potting up cover the bulb completely with soil to 2.4cm (¼ inch) below soil level. New leaves should begin to appear in about two weeks. If you have left your plant in its pot over the winter period, remove all dead leaves and place the plant in a sunny position and increase your watering.

During summer Venus Fly Traps grow best in a temperature range of 15 to 30 Degrees C. (60 to 85 degrees F.). Reducing this range of 15 degrees to a range of 18 to 25 degrees C. will usually produce a bigger and healthier plant, as will increasing the amount of daylight hours.

Venus Fly Traps respond to grow-lux globes or tubes quite well. The plants can be grown with a photo period of eight to

Dionaea Muscipula 21

Venus Fly Trap

twelve hours in winter and twelve to sixteen in summer.

While there are still many people debating whether this plant or that plant is carnivorous, the most controversial issue amongst growers themselves is the type of soil to use. The type of soil recommended for Venus Fly Traps ranges from straight sphagnum moss to straight peat moss, and in between variations such as half peat and half sphagnum; half peat and half scoria; half peat, one-quarter scoria and one-quarter sphagnum. The difference between the various mixes and their effectiveness depends on the method of watering, size of pot, growing conditions and age of plant. I have found the best all round and easy to make up mix is three-quarter peat and one-quarter vermiculite.

Vermiculite is magnesium-aluminium-iron silicate heated to 2,000 degrees F. This causes the thin layers of the mineral to pop, resulting in a sponge-like, light substance that supplies plants with magnesium and potassium, while also aerating the soil.

Peat moss (or moss peat as it is sometimes called) is highly acidic (PH 3.8 to 7.0) and is simply the remains of sphagnum moss preserved over a period of time under water in swamps or bogs.

Most types of Carnivorous Plants are found in swamps or bogs where the nutrition in the soil is low. These plants gain their nutrition from the insects that exist in these areas. Because they are native to these sorts of areas, they are of course accustomed to extremely moist soils.

Using tap water to keep the soil moist for your Carnivorous Plants can cause a build-up of salts, etc. It is therefore recommended that rain water or distilled water be used at all times with these plants.

If you can't get distilled water or rain water then either boil up the tap water and allow it to cool before use; otherwise allow some tap water to stand for at least twenty-four hours before using.

Venus Fly Traps usually die because growers either continually spring the traps, force feed the plant or water with tap water. If you have to use tap water then it is advisable to re-pot your plant each year into fresh peat moss to prevent a build up of salts. If after this you still don't have much success then consider growing your plant in a terrarium (see Chapter 14) or in some form of glass or plastic container. Terraria require little attention and therefore little can go wrong.

4

Pitcher Plants (*Sarracenia*)

*T*hese plants are passive Carnivores, which is to say the insect is attracted to the pitcher by its smell and colour, and it then proceeds to move down the pitcher, past downward-pointing hairs. While it is a smooth trip going down, the hairs (or spikes) make it impossible for the insect to travel back upwards.

Towards the base of the pitcher the plant secretes an enzyme which dissolves the insect and sends the nourishment, in the form of amino acids, peptides and other nutrients from the insect to various areas in the plant.

As can be seen from the photo insects build up inside the pitcher, each attracted by the smell of the plant itself and that of

Distribution of Sarracenia ▼

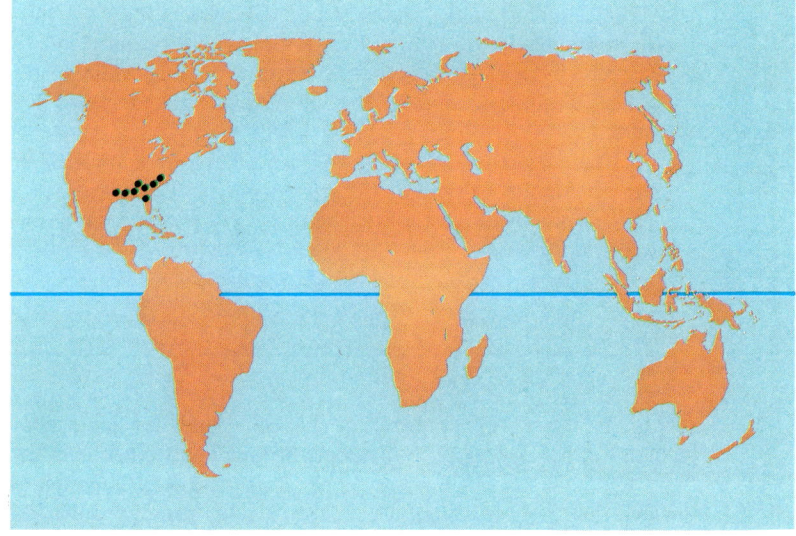

the other insects rotting in the pitcher. The amount of insects in a pitcher can also be seen by holding the plant to the light and observing the darker area towards the base of the plant. The smell of decaying insects is similar to that of rotting meat, although the fumes aren't obvious unless the pitcher is actually cut open. So if you grow them in a glass house you will not be driven away by any unpleasant smell.

The *Sarracenia* Genus has eight species or varieties and many more hybrids. Species include *Alata, Flava, Leucophylla, Minor, Oreophylla, Psittacina, Purpurea* and *Rubra*.

This Genus is very popular amongst Carnivorous Plant growers because all species can be hybridised, or cross pollinated as it is more commonly called. Each grower can invent her or his own new variety. Many of the hybrids do of course occur naturally in the peat bogs where they originate; but due to the geographical distance between certain species and the fact that they don't all flower at the same time, many hybrids would not occur at all if it weren't for the collector artfully collecting pollen from one plant and fertilizing another.

Some of the most interesting and exciting plants (including the *Willasii x Leucophylla* on the cover) have developed in this way. For the grower it is an exciting time waiting for the seeds to grow; having some inkling how the plant will turn out, but never knowing for sure.

Many of the plants in the Genus grow in swampy areas which are flooded during certain times of the year, and frozen at others. For example, I have seen Sarracenia Purpurea covered with water up to 10 centimetres (4 inches) above the plant, for a couple of months without any adverse effects; while species like Oreophylla can tolerate drier conditions with increased heat in summer.

This Genus is very hardy and can be grown in most of the range of conditions each of the species is found in. Therefore it is only necessary to give a brief description of each plant and its general habitat.

Species

SARRACENIA ALATA

This plant is native to Texas in the USA, and has light yellow petals to the flowers. The pitchers are long and tubular and have a rounded lid and a few red veins. There is a Red Throat form which has a deep burgundy colour inside, running down the pitcher. More common is the light green form, and this grows to about sixty centimetres, (two feet).

SARRACENIA FLAVA

This plant differs from Alata in that the hood seems to have been pinched at the back, forming a waisted look. The throat itself is a crimson colour. Flava is often more yellow than Alata, although again there is diversity within this species and both dark green and deep red forms can be found. Native to Georgia in the USA this species grows to a height of one metre, (39 inches), and is therefore taller than Alata. The petals are light yellow to green. The centres, or pistils, are light green in colour.

SARRACENIA MINOR

This plant is common to the south-east of the USA and has pitchers seldom exceeding 60 centimetres (24 inches) which makes it a shorter plant than the Alata, Flava or Leucophylla; but still very interesting, with its rounded hood and white patches. In full sunlight this plant, as with the Sarracenia Oreophylla, takes on a brownish red tinge towards the top of the pitcher. The rim of the pitcher is usually burgundy coloured and has droplets of nectar secreted all around it. It is this nectar that attracts insects, especially ants, to the plant. Once insects have arrived at the rim and start sampling the nectar, they are under the shadow of the lid, with much of the light coming from the front and lower end of the pitcher. These two factors, the insect's desire for more food, and the light that comes in from all angles, invite the prey to venture down the tube. Insects then get confused, lost, and eventually trapped.

The flower of the *Sarracenia Minor* has yellow petals; these appear on a stem just below the pitcher. This species usually requires less water than the other sarracenias. The pitchers may stay on the plant over winter and not die off as on the Sarracenia Oreophylla.

SARRACENIA OREOPHYLLA

This species usually loses all its pitchers over the winter period, leaving the plant with winter leaves, called Phyllodia. These winter leaves are non-carnivorous and will appear only in mature plants. They die off with the emergence of spring, as the pitchers start to appear. I have found this species the hungriest of all the Sarracenia, with pitchers so full that they eventually fall over with the weight. Each of these pitchers will eventually rot, to be replaced by another pitcher, bigger and better than the last. *Oreophylla* is often confused with Sarracenia Flava, but there are distinct differences between the two. The Oreophylla has shorter pitchers of about sixty cm (24 inches) compared to the Flava's longer pitchers. The Oreophylla also is fatter at the top with a lid that doesn't overhang to the same extent as it does in the Flava. The inside of the pitcher has fine red veins on the neck of the lid running down to the base of the pitcher. Flava on the other hand has dark veins on the neck, when veining does occur, and few, if any, travelling down the pitcher. Petals on the Oreophylla are light green and the Phyllodia curve back at the top instead of remaining straight, as in the case of the Flava.

It is best not to stand Oreophylla in water over winter, and to water less than most Sarracenia during summer.

SARRACENIA LEUCOPHYLLA

Leucophylla is one of the most striking of the tall Sarracenias, with its white throat and red veins going down to a green base. This, together with its ruffled lid and extreme height, growing to one metre (39 inches), makes it a very attractive plant and an excellent species to hybridise with. A large field of this plant looks like a mass of tall thin leaves with snow white tops, and when in flower the scene is scattered with deep burgundy petals.

I have often seen mosquitos attempt to suck blood from the red veins on this plant. In due course they proceed down the pitcher, never to be seen again.

Often on mature plants of about five years, the petals are burgundy in colour on tall stems, slightly longer than the pitchers.

SARRACENIA PSITTACINA

Pitchers on this species initially grow straight up, then as the top becomes fatter and redder it falls back to lie horizontally on the surface of the soil. It is for this reason that I usually use a wider and shallower pot for *Psittacinas* than for other Sarracenias. Over time the pitchers become quite fat and more rounded at the tip. As sunlight is increased the green pitchers change colour from a light green to burgundy, making the white spots stand out

Sarracenia Leucophylla ▲

even more. With increased watering and sunlight the pitchers should become redder, shorter and fatter, instead of thin, tall and green as they are often found in the wild.

Even though the pitchers lie flat and usually don't grow larger than 25mm (10 inches) their shape and colour make this a very attractive plant.

Sarracenia
▲ *Psittacina*

Like the Minor this plant has windows of light which confuse the insect, once it has entered the pitcher. Once inside light is coming into the pitcher from all angles, making this pitcher appear like a mirror maze, without any obvious exit. Eventually the prey finds its way along the pitcher, past the forward-pointing hairs to find itself trapped at the base of the plant.

This plant likes large amounts of water, and it is often seen submerged in water during the flooding season without any adverse effect. Some botanists even suggest the plant catches more insects when covered with water than when growing above the water line. This together with the fact that exit from the forward-pointing hairs is impossible, explains why the plant is often called the "lobster pot". Sarracenia Purpurea is also often flooded but there is no evidence that it gains nourishment through being in this state.

SARRACENIA PURPUREA

Forms of *Purpurea* can be dark burgundy in colour with no hint of green, or totally green, as in the sub species Heterophylla, without a hint of red.

It is difficult to generalise about this particular plant as there are commonly considered to be two different types of Purpurea. Firstly, there is the Sarracenia Purpurea Purpurea Heterophylla. This species is all green, as shown in the photograph on page 32. Heterophylla is simply a different form of Purpurea Purpurea, and should correctly be called Sarracenia Purpurea ssp. Purpurea Heterophylla. For reasons of simplicity we shall refer to it as the Heterophylla. The Sarracenia Purpurea Purpurea can have both burgundy and burgundy to green pitchers. The hood is not as ruffled and it is usually thinner than the third type, the Purpurea Venosa. The Purpurea Purpurea is difficult to distinguish from the Heterophylla, when the former is grown in shade. But it is easy to distinguish between Purpurea Purpurea and Purpurea Venosa as the latter has an obvious ruffled hood and wider pitchers. I consider the Venosa the most attractive of the three, and refer mainly to this variety of Purpurea in my general description.

This plant's attractiveness lies in the shape of the deep burgundy, bulbous pitchers, which grow up to 10cm (4 inches) across, and have a ruffled hood with the ever present downward pointing hairs. These features have made this plant very popular as a plant to create hybrids with.

Recent literature has suggested that each Sarracenia species attracts its own select group of insects. Sarracenia Minor appears to have ants as its main diet. The Sarracenia Purpurea certainly seems to uphold this theory, as I have noticed that its prey consists almost entirely of slaters. Slaters seem to fill the pitcher almost to overflowing, never appearing to be perturbed by the fact that other slaters have obviously met their death in the very same pitcher.

The Purpurea forms a cluster of pitchers around the base of the plant, which is known as the rhyzome. As the rhyzome increases in size the plant forms another centre and hence another plant. This new cluster can be removed from the rhyzome and potted up, as mentioned above.

As with other Sarracenias, this plant flowers in spring, and has deep red petals on a stem usually no larger than about 30cm (12 inches).

After about four years the plant is usually mature enough to flower, and a quite small plant can have two or more flower

▲ *Sarracenia Purpurea ssp. Venosa*

stems. A mature plant can be defined as one with about ten pitchers, each about six inches long.

A QUICK GUIDE TO PURPUREA SUB SPECIES:

Pitchers Green only .... *Heterophylla*
Pitchers green to burgundy, filled hood, short and fat. . . . *Venosa*
Pitchers green to burgundy, without filled hood, long and narrow .... *Purpurea*

SARRACENIA RUBRA

Like the Purpurea this species has a number of varieties that have caused considerable controversy. The sub species have been named *Rubra Rubra, Rubra Jonesii, Rubra Gulfensis, Rubra Alabamensis* and *Rubra Wherryi*.

The first spring pitchers of the Rubra vary from the later season pitchers; this together with the fact that each of the sub species varies in such characteristics as height and thickness makes identification extremely difficult. With the Purpurea it is possible to distinguish between the different types. The differences are obvious: not merely a pitcher being thicker or thinner, but also the presence or absence of such features as colour, frills, or red veins. With the Rubra the difference is marginal and relies mainly on size and thickness of the pitcher. With this in mind it is possible to order the plants in terms of height and thickness. The tallest is Rubra Gulfensis (or Gulf Coast) at 68cm (25 inches) which is not as wide as the Rubra Jonesii, but both are taller than Rubra Rubra. This plant has generally thinner pitchers, although this can depend on the environment in which the plant is grown. Rubra Alabamensis is a short, stocky plant with a large lid overhanging the pitcher. The smallest Rubra, the Wherryi, is redder than Alabamensis but otherwise quite similar. Rubra Rubra grows to a height of about 35cm. (14 inches) and the other plants group themselves around this height.

The Rubra species seems to flower quite readily. With only four pitchers, each 20cm high (8 inches), the plant will send up a flower, usually quite small and with red coloured petals. The pitchers generally have a reddish brown tinge throughout.

Sarracenia Rubra ssp. Rubra ◄

DIVISION OF

Sarracenia Purpurea ssp. Purpurea F. Heterophylla

Sarracenias can be reproduced by seed, leaf cutting or rhyzome splitting. Seed should be sprinkled on live sphagnum moss, watered in, then covered with clear plastic to aid germination. After the seedlings have reached a size of 2 — 5 cm

Sarracenia Purpurea ssp. Purpurea F. Heterophylla with large rhyzome ready to divide into three plants

SARRACENIA RHYZOME

(1—2 inches), they can be planted up into small pots.

Leaf cuttings can be obtained by using a sharp knife to remove the healthy leaves from the base of the plant, ensuring that the white section that attaches the leaf to the rhyzome is included. The base of this leaf cutting should be dipped into a rooting hormone, then placed in sphagnum moss. Cover the plant with plastic and in time roots will develop and the plant can be potted up.

The most successful method of reproduction is by rhyzome cutting. To cut the rhyzome, split it in such a way that roots are still remaining on each section. As can be seen in Figure Two, a sharp knife is used to cut this rhyzome in three sections. Each of these has its own root system, as seen in Figure Three. Even if the rhyzome doesn't have roots the plant will still reproduce, if the rhyzome is big enough (over say ½ inch) and sufficient care is taken. Each of the new plants is then potted up as shown in Figure Four, and then watered.

Fig.3

Sarracenia divisions each plant divided ▲

Fig.4

Sarracenia divisions potted up

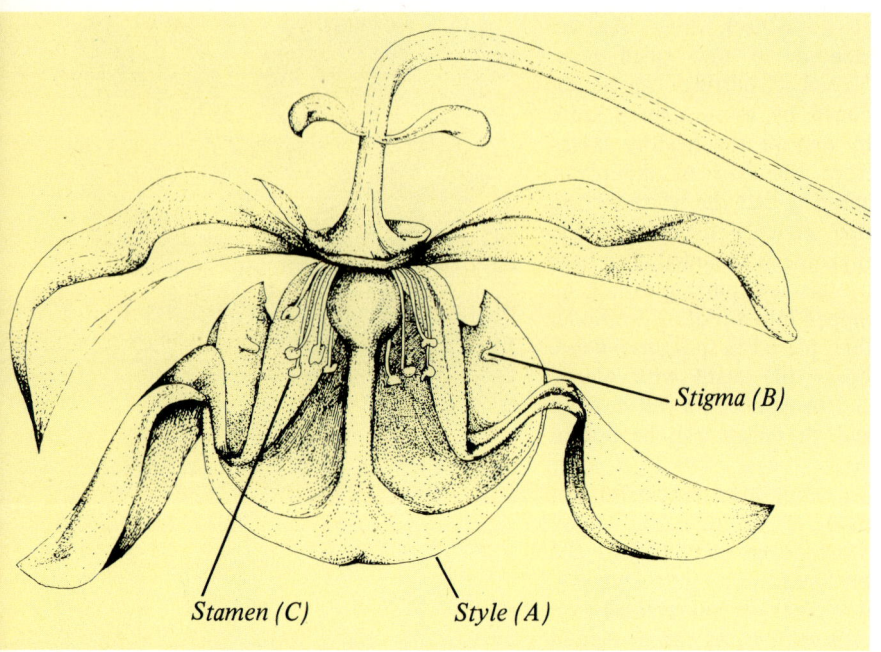

Side view of Sarracenia ▲ flower

HYBRIDIZING

To create a Sarracenia hybrid you will need two small paint brushes and flowers from two different Sarracenia species. Under each flower you will find an umbrella-like shape, upside down, called the style (A) which has five points stigmas (B). The petals will droop between these points. The umbrella will collect pollen as it falls from the stamens (C). Pollen, a yellow to white coloured powder, can be found by lifting up the petal.

With one paint brush get the pollen from the first flower and brush the stigma of the second flower, label the brush and put it aside. With the other paint brush, get the pollen from the second flower and brush this on the stigma of the first flower.

Using two different brushes prevents the plants from self-pollinating, which would only give you seeds of the two plants you already have.

Continue this procedure each day until the flowers fade. If one plant appears to start flowering ahead of the other plant, put the early flower in a cooler position to retard its growth.

If you can't get both plants to flower together, it is possible to store pollen in a plastic bag (away from light) for a little while.

Sarracenia

Sarracenia Hybrid *Willasii* x *Leucophylla*

36 Sarracenia

Sarracenia Areolata, Hybrid Alata x Leucophylla ▲

SARRACENIA SPECIES AND HYBRIDS

Where only one name is written after "S" the variety is a species; where there is more than one name it is either a sub species or a hybrid.

- S. Ahlesii = *Alata x Rubra*
- S. Alata
- S. Areolata = *Alata x Leucophylla*
- S. Cantabridgiensis = *Leucophylla x Minor*
- S. Catesbaei = *Flava x Purpurea*
- S. Chelsonii = *Purpurea x Rubra*
- S. Courtii = *Psittacina x Purpurea*
- S. Diesneriana = *Courtii x Flava*
- S. Drummondii = *S. Leucophylla*
- S. Evendine = *Catesbaei x Leucophylla*
- S. Excellens = *Leucophylla x Minor*
- S. Exornata = *Alata x Purpurea*
- S. Farnhamii = *Leucophylla x Rubra*
- S. Flava
- S. Formosa = *Minor x Psittacina*
- S. Gilpini = *Psittacina x Rubra*
- S. Harperi = *Flava x Minor*
- S. Illustrata = *Alata x Catesbaei*
- S. Laschkei = *Courtii x Mooreana*
- S. Leucophylla
- S. Marston Mill = *(Leucophylla x Catesbaei) x Flava*
- S. Melanorhoda = *Catesbaei x Purpurea*
- S. Minor
- S. Mitchelliana = *Leucophylla x Purpurea*
- S. Mooreana = *Flava x Leucophylla*
- S. Oreophylla
- S. Popei = *Flava x Rubra*
- S. Psittacina
- S. Purpurea Gibbosa = *S. Purpurea ssp. purpurea*
- S. Purpurea ssp. Purpurea Form Heterophylla
- S. Purpurea ssp. Purpurea
- S. Purpurea ssp. Venosa
- S. Readii = *Leucophylla x Rubra*
- S. Rehderi = *Minor x Rubra*
- S. Rubra ssp. Alabamensis
- S. Rubra ssp. Gulfensis
- S. Rubra ssp. Jonesii
- S. Rubra ssp. Rubra
- S. Rubra ssp. Wherryi
- S. Sanderiana = *Leucophylla x Readii*
- S. Sledgei = *S. Alata*
- S. Swaniana = *Minor x Purpurea*
- S. Vetteriana = *Illustrata x Catesbaei*
- S. Vittata Maculata = *Purpurea x Chelsonii*
- S. Vogeliana = *Courtii x Catesbaei*
- S. Willisii = *Courtii x Melanorhoda*
- S. Wrigleyana = *Leucophylla x Psittacina*

NOTE

ssp. refers to sub species of the same species, for example Venosa is a sub species of Purpurea.

x refers to plants that have been crossed or hybridized, for example Alata crossed with Rubra becomes Alata x Rubra.

Albany Pitcher Plant
(Cephalotus Follicularis)

This plant is commonly called the Albany Pitcher Plant as it is native to the west side of Australia, growing near a town called Albany. This town has a maximum summer temperature of 90 degrees C. (105 F.) and minimum water temperature of 5 degrees C. (42 F.).

This plant grows near slow flowing creeks and is native to this particular area in Western Australia only, as can be seen from the map. Plants can be found in cattle farms, with pitchers being trampled on regularly; much of the area also undergoes selective burning every few years. Even with all these hazards to its existence, the *Cephalotus* seems to continue to survive, nonetheless its numbers are slowly decreasing year by year.

Distribution of Cephalotus ▼ *Follicularis*

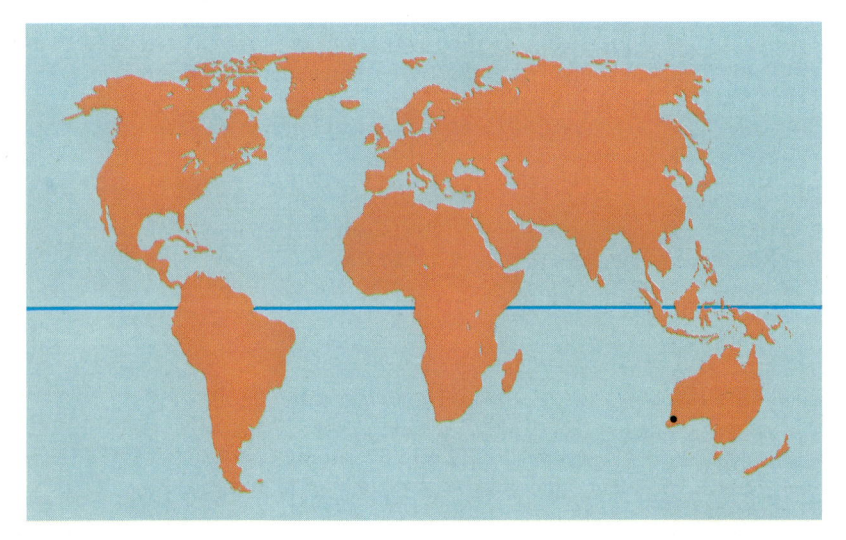

Cephalotus Follicularis in its natural habitat ▲

Although this plant is often called a pitcher plant, this generalisation is hardly accurate, as can be seen from the photograph and when it is compared to the Sarracenia.

Cephalotus has a very thick, woody root running in all directions in the peat and sphagnum moss in which it grows wild. This means that even when the pitchers are squashed, or dried out due to heat, the deep root system can stay quite damp and next season the plant will come back with renewed vigour.

While it looks as though it is ready for dinner, its lid always being wide open, this plant is not an active carnivore. However, this doesn't detract from its interesting trapping mechanism. As insects (mainly ants), crawl over the red ribs and past the rim, towards the sweet smelling nectar zone, they lose their footing and fall into the pitcher, which is filled with water.

Because the ribs overhang the sides of the pitcher like teeth, they make it impossible for an insect to crawl out again. Eventually an insect is dissolved by the digestive juices the plant secretes.

Flying insects are attracted by the plant's own nectar to the pitcher. It is said that once under the lid they see the reflection of light through the lid onto the well of liquid. They become confused about which way is up and dive into the water, to meet the same fate as the ants.

▶Close up of Cephalotus Follicularis

Therefore, this ingenious plant has developed a method to trap both crawling and flying insects, using both light and slippery surfaces; and yet its pitchers are no bigger than 5cm (2 inches). Under ideal conditions pitchers may grow up to 10cm (4 inches) with the help of artificial light and high humidity, but they seldom reach this size in the wild.

During the winter the plant produces normal, non-carnivorous leaves from the crown. If the plant is kept outside then these non-carnivorous leaves, which are dark green in colour and waxy in appearance, will usually develop in Spring, together with the flowers.

Upon first sight, the flower stem appears to be just another pitcher, until it keeps on growing. As the stem reaches 30cm (12 inches) in height the flower pod thickens, and the flower usually opens when the stem has reached 45cm (18 inches). However, I have seen one plant under a bench send up a 90cm (36 inch) stem running up the wall of the glass house, and eventually flower when it reached the light.

The flowers themselves are quite small, only about one cm wide (¼ inch), with no petals; really quite unimpressive. Though difficult to generalise, a plant would usually need at least six large pitchers and a main root of about 10cm (4 inches) long before it will flower.

CARE

Growing the plant by seed has been met with varied success. Other methods, such as leaf and root cuttings, have been very successful.

In time Cephalotus clumps become quite thick and require thinning. Often when thinning a plant's leaves, pitchers and even

Cephalotus Follicularis with main tap root showing and new shoots that can be removed and potted up ◄

roots will break off. These can be planted in peat moss, sprayed with a fungicide, covered with a plastic bag and left for at least eight weeks, then the plastic should be removed. After a couple of months new shoots should begin to appear. Spray again with a fungicide, then leave in a protected position. These cuttings can be potted up after about six months, by which time the plant

Cephalotus Folicularis grown from root cuttings ▲

should have four pitchers as well as non-carnivorous leaves.

If the root cutting is very small, under 12mm (½ inch), then only small pitchers will develop at first, and in time more and more will appear, but all remaining below 12mm. If the root cutting is over one inch then less pitchers will appear, but each of these will be 12 to 25 mm (½ to one inch) long.

Cephalotus are best watered from a tray all year round, although in summer a light misting will reduce the leaf surface temperature. The plant grows naturally in tall grass and as such is accustomed to filtered light. If this light is too dark then the pitchers will stay green. As sunlight increases the pitcher's rim will start to turn burgundy in colour, as will the lid. If sunlight is increased, together with more humidity, then the pitchers may turn almost black.

While Cephalotus can survive quite well with little light, it looks far more attractive as it takes on the burgundy colour.

6

Sun Pitchers (*Heliamphora*)

*T*he *Heliamphora* is still one of the rarest Genera of the Carnivorous Plant species, and one of which little is known. The Genus has six species to date, and all are native to Venzuala and grow on top of high mountain plateaux.

To get to the high plateaux requires boating up the Amazon River, trekking through the jungle and finally climbing up the edge of the mountains, past an area commonly called the slime forest, because of its mosses and extreme dampness, not to mention leeches.

One of the things that makes this plant of such great interest to Carnivorous Plant growers is that it is believed by some

Distribution of Heliamphora ▼

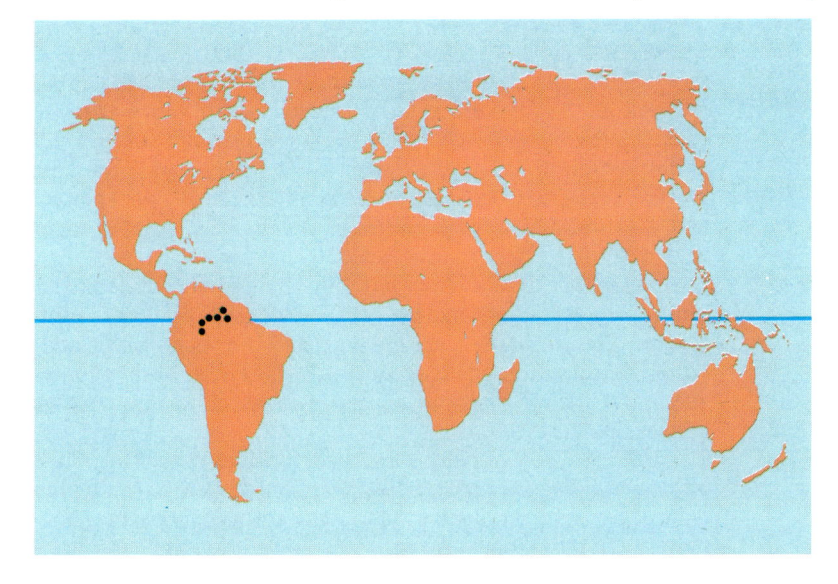

Heliamphora Heterodoxa with new pitchers coming up

to be the primitive link between pitcher plants and "normal" leaves. since the area in which it was found has been frozen in time due to its isolation from other land masses and the usual process of evolution.

These great plateaux were once on a great land mass, believed to be the oldest in existence, which was eventually eroded away by water courses, leaving the plateaux isolated and an inspiration to Sir Arthur Conan Doyle in his book "The Lost World". Many areas of these plateaux are still largely unexplored, and may well reveal more species of Carnivorous Plants in times to come.

You will notice from the photographs that the pitcher looks like a leaf which has had its sides pressed together to form a seam. This structure stops the pitcher from filling with water, becoming top heavy and consequently falling over. Many pitchers also have a slit further down the seam which acts as another drainage point.

The leaves look very waxy and feel like fine velvet. They have a trapping mechanism like Sarracenias; that is to say the inner surface of the pitcher has downward pointing hairs which prevent the prey from escaping.

The little cap at the top of the pitcher is usually red and loses colour when the light is decreased. The flowers on the Heterodoxa are initially white, then like the rim and the cap, turn red in time. Flowers on all the three cultivated species look like orchids with two or more on each of the long stems.

SPECIES

Of the six known species — *Heterodoxa, Macdonaldae, Minor, Nutans, Tatei* and *Tyleri* — only three are at present in cultivation. These are the Heterodoxa, from Mt. Mari-Tepui; the Minor, from Mt. Auyan-Tepui; and Nutans, from Mt. Roraima. The Heterodoxa is the largest with pitchers growing to 30cm (12 inches).

CARE

Due to the low numbers in cultivation the exact requirements of this rare Genus are still uncertain. From my own limited experience and that of other growers, some generalisations can be made: the Heliamphora doesn't like extremes of temperature, and ideally should be grown within a range of 13 degrees C. and 24 degrees C. (55° F. and 75 F.).

One method I have found effective is to pot the plant into straight sphagnum moss and place this pot on top of a layer of sphagnum moss, inside a terrarium. Now the terrarium can be placed in a heated propagating tray. Above the terrarium, at a height of about 25cm (10 inches) a grow light should operate on a twelve hour cycle per day.

Every few days, water is passed through the plant. If the edges of the pitchers begin to turn brown, or the leaves begin to wrinkle slightly, the plant is probably too dry. While this plant does like being well watered it also prefers good drainage, and as a consequence you may find the plant grows better when the sphagnum is mixed with perlite. While perlite or Scoria provides no minerals to the soil it does help in the aeration of the mixture.

Sundews
(Drosera)

There are about one hundred known species of this Genus, about half of which are native to Australia. These plants range from the short and flat *Drosera Hamiltoni* to the tall and stringy *Drosera Gigantea* which grows up to 100cm (two feet) tall.

One characteristic common to all Drosera is the tentacles on the leaves which have droplets of water containing a sticky substance at the tip. It is these droplets of water which with their sticky substance hold the insect and eventually dissolve the prey, sending nourishment to the rest of the plant.

As the insect lands on one of the tentacles and gets stuck

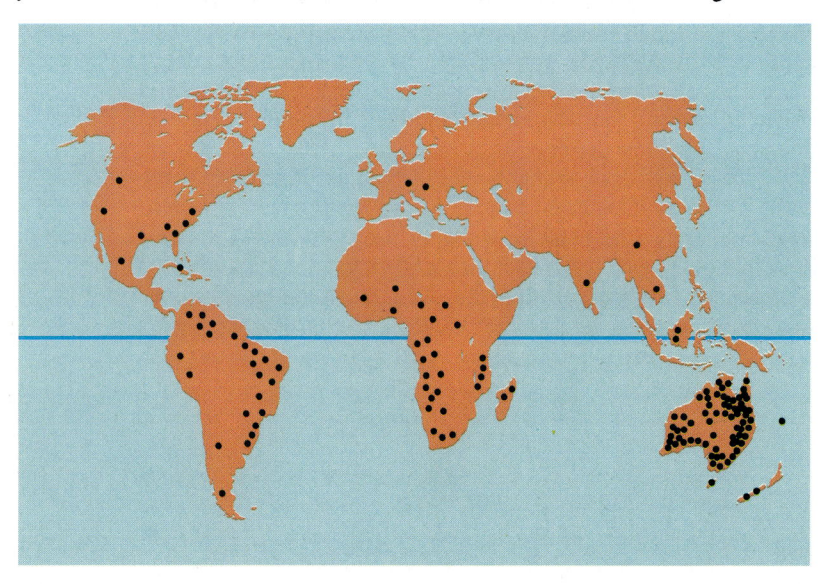

Distribution ▼ of Drosera

Drosera Adelae ▲

more tentacles move to grab the prey; eventually the whole leaf may roll up and engulf the insect. Over time the digestive enzyme in each of the tentacles dissolves the soft part of the body of the insect, the leaf unrolls and the hard shell remains to be blown away.

Species

DROSERA ADELAE

Adelae is native to North Australia and exists in marshy creek areas. This plant has quite long and thin leaves which grow to 20cm (8 inches). While basically green in colour the leaves can appear to have a burgundy tinge due to the many reddish-burgundy tentacles on each leaf and the pale burgundy rib running the length of each leaf.

Each plant may have one or more flower stems which grow up to 30cm (12 inches) tall. The flower stem has ten or more flowers with small inconspicuous petals of a light brown colour. While this plant does quite well in filtered light and is therefore

48   *Drosera*

suitable for indoor terraria, increased light results in darker green to wine coloured leaves, which I find more appealing. As this Drosera is native to the constantly warm climate of Northern Australia it is not suitable to be grown outside in areas that experience frost.

DROSERA BINATA

This is quite a tall plant with leaf stalks up to 30cm (12 inches). Towards the top of the leaf can be found a fork, which forms the letter "Y".

Numerous white petalled flowers appear in late spring and early summer.

The *Binata*, like many Australian Drosera, goes into winter dormancy. This simply means that the portion of the plant lying above the soil will dry up, or die and rot off, leaving the base of the plant, the root system, still intact. The top part of the plant will re-emerge next season.

Drosera Erythror- ▼ *hiza*

Binata is found in damp, boggy areas where the temperature can drop to zero, and is therefore suitable for a peat garden.

DROSERA ERYTHRORHIZA

The *Erythrorhiza* is native to West Australia and comes up in dry sandy soil during Autumn. This plant is one of the tuberous Droseras which means that it goes into dormancy during the summer. It experiences dry hot conditions with temperatures in the range of 25–30 degrees C. (80–85 degrees F.).

Erythrorhiza is one of the largest rosette sundews; so big it could cover a hand with its olive green leaves of 10cm (4 inches) across. The tuber is 1–2 cm (½ to ¾ inch) across.

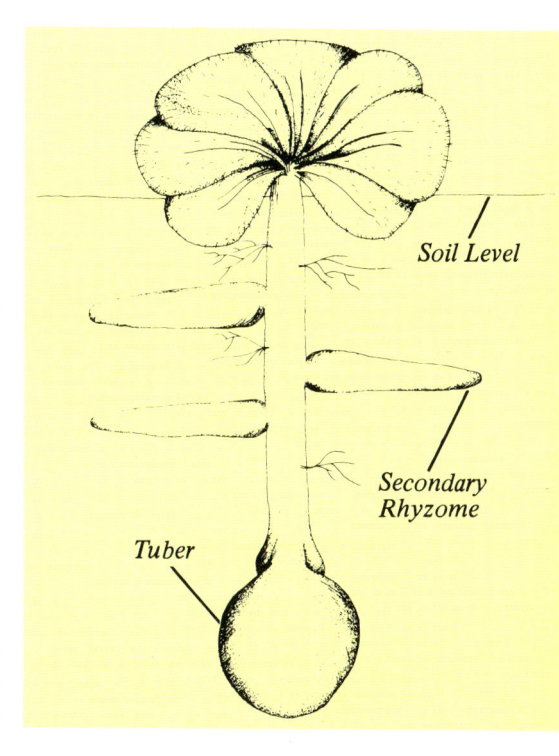

Drosera Erythrorhiza: Side view of root system of tuberous *Drosera* ▲

Three or more white petalled flowers may appear on a single stem during autumn, often after a fire when growing wild. If you want your plant to flower then consider burning leaves etc. on top of the pot during summer, although this can cause the plant to flower before any leaves appear and often exhaust the plant.

Well drained sandy soil in a large 8 inch pot is required. A good soil mix is three parts sand and one part peat moss. Allow the plant to dry out gradually over spring, until it reaches a completely dry state for summer, otherwise the tuber will rot.

This plant also forms secondary rhyzomes as can be seen in the drawing. Often when the plant is potted other rosettes will form around the inside of the pot, pushed against the side. These can be taken off the parent plant and re-potted; they attain mature size in a couple of seasons.

DROSERA GIGANTEA

As its name implies, this is one of the biggest of the Drosera. *Drosera Gigantea* grows in the shape of a tree, with a sturdy main stem and many smaller stems branching off. At intervals along the smaller branches are more stems, on the tips of which are the cup shaped leaves with tentacles. Its flowers are white and appear in spring. They grow off the branches which stem from the main stem.

Gigantea is native to West Australia where it grows in sandy, peat soil, and may easily rot if it hasn't sufficient drainage.

DROSERA CISTIFLORA

Like the Binata this plant also goes into dormancy, forming a rhyzome to survive the drier weather. It has very long, thin, light green leaves of about five cm (2 inches) branching from a single thick stem of about 30cm (12 inches) tall. The plant's overall appearance is a pink to light green colour with white flowers on top.

The plant grows in sandy, peat soils, and is native to South Africa. There are a total of eighteen species native to South Africa; other species include Hilaris, Trinervia and Regia, to name a few.

DROSERA HAMILTONI

The *Hamiltoni* is one of the rosette type of Drosera, and has flat, green to burgundy leaves radiating from the centre of the plant. The Hamiltoni is often found alongside the Cephalotus Folicularis in quite swampy areas. It has dark pink to purple flowers, which often grow up to 30cm (12 inches) in height.

Like the Cephalotus the Hamiltoni only grows in limited localities, and is also becoming rare. Hamiltoni has a similar root system to the Cephalotus in that it has a long thick root which can be cut up and planted. These root sections are about 2.5cm (one inch) long, and should be planted in a soil mix of peat and sand. New plants should begin to appear in three months.

DROSERA PELTATA

The *Drosera Peltata* has a dormant tuber at the base of its root system. This makes it possible for the plant to go into dormancy during the hot summer months when the soil is very dry, and appear again in autumn as the ground becomes moist. Peltata is widespread in each of the six states of Australia.

The Peltata grows to a height of 30cm (12 inches) but at this height it usually relies on thin grass or another Peltata for support. It has many white flowers which appear on the main stem in the spring. Also off this main stem are branches of one to three cm (½ inch), at the tips of which are the characteristic cupped leaves with their sticky tentacles.

Drosera Peltata in its natural habitat as it emerges from summer dormancy

Inset: Drosera Peltata ▲

DROSERA PYGMAEA

As the name suggests this plant is one of the smallest of the Drosera, little bigger than a one cent coin (2 cm — ¾ inch). Although small this plant is quite prolific and if put in a terrarium it spreads so quickly that within a couple of seasons it has spread like a reddish carpet to cover the soil.

Small white flowers rise to about twice the size of the plant in late spring to early summer.

While no single plant can catch a large insect, I have seen quite large insects trapped by large areas of these Drosera.

Habitat of Drosera Whittakerii

Inset: Close up of Drosera ▲ *Whittakerii*

DROSERA WHITTAKERII

Like the Peltata this plant resorts to a dormant tuber in summer, and re-emerges again in autumn. This sundew is also of the rosette type, with leaves up to two cm (one inch) radiating from the centre. Its flowers, when in full bloom, are so large that they almost cover the whole plant. There are often two or more flowers on the stems. The stems themselves grow to about four cm. (1½ inches).

CARE

The Whittakerii is a very hardy Drosera with leaves quite thick and leathery. As with many of the tuberous Drosera the plant should be allowed to dry out over summer. When the autumn period arrives stand the pot in water for a few days, then keep the plant moist. The plant should start to appear in about two weeks. Full sunlight can cause the green leaves to take on a reddish tinge, but the plant seems to grow bigger when given filtered light and kept cool, ideally 5 degrees C. (42 F.) winter temperature during the night, and 15 degrees C. (60 F.) during the day.

A sign of a healthy drosera is one that has droplets of water on each of the tentacles. Often these will disappear during the extreme heat periods of the day and then re-appear as the day becomes cooler towards evening. For many Drosera this is their natural condition. But if the droplets are not present even at night then the plant is probably lacking in water or humidity or both. If you notice your plant looking a bit dry then cover with a glass jar, plastic bag, etc. till the droplets re-appear. This should take a few hours. Water the plant well and move it to a better location.

Of the one hundred or so species of sundews about half of these are native to Australia. There are far too many to mention here but a few of quite different appearances are worth naming. These are the *Adelae, Petiolaris, Schizandra, Spathulata* and *Zonaria.*

8

Hanging Pitcher Plants
(Nepenthes)

Once again this genus is gaining in popularity. In Victorian times it was quite common to see *Nepenthes* in what were then called "stove houses". In fact so common were these plants that "Cassels Popular Gardening" of the 1800s describes how to propogate such species as Nepenthes Albo-Maginata, Nepenthes Rajah and Nepenthes Sanguinea; all considered to be very rare today.

This genus with its seventy species and many more hybrids is essentially tropical and as such requires high humidity and warm weather to produce good pitchers. Once these conditions are met then the pitchers can be quite large.

Distribution
▼ *of Nepenthes*

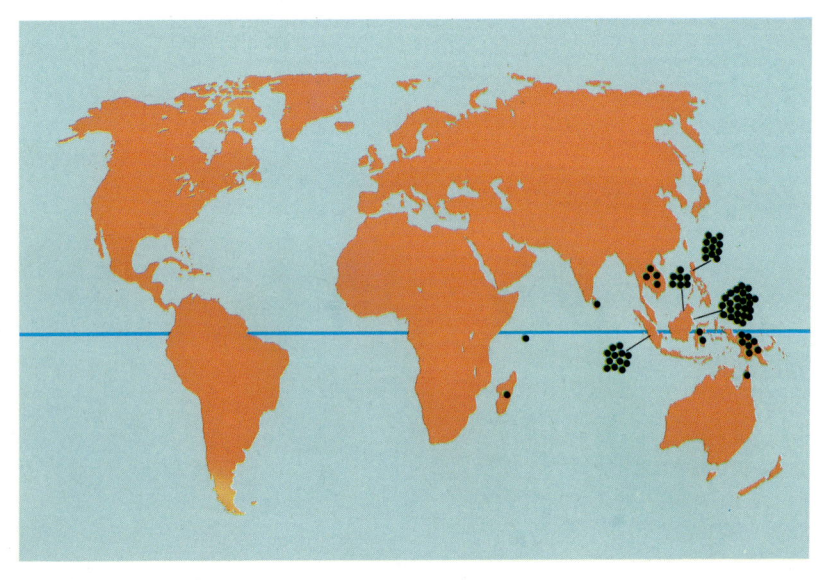

Nepenthes have been put to some very interesting uses, for instance, natives in tropical areas managed to use this plant to carry water, and some tribes used the sterile liquid from unopened pitchers to care for inflamed eyes (*Nepenthes* by Danser). Still other natives cooked rice in the pitchers.

Highland Nepenthes are those plants that are native to altitudes greater than 1,000 metres (.6 of a mile). This simply means that the plants grow in an area above the jungle canopies, and while experiencing quite bright and warm day time temperatures, the night temperature is quite cool, often as low as 5 degrees C. At high altitudes many Nepenthes grow in total fog almost all the time, while others emerge from the fog at midday, only to be covered again in late afternoon.

It is this unusual feature of cool nights that has made these highland species very rare in cultivation, which is unfortunate as the highland species are among the most attractive Nepenthes. They include such species as Rajah, Villosa, Edwardsiana, Lowii, Fusca, Pervillei, Spectabilis and Ventricosa, to name a few of the most eye catching. Beginners should avoid the highland species as they are the most difficult to grow.

In many Nepenthes species the lower pitchers are usually fatter and shorter and appear quite different from the upper pitchers, which are generally narrower and longer. This can make identification quite difficult, especially when for years you have been used to seeing only the lower pitchers of a particular plant. This has in fact caused many species to be misnamed. There is often a mistaken belief among growers that Nepenthes need to be tall to have very big pitchers. This isn't at all the case as mature pitchers can form on many of the species when the plant is no bigger than 30cm (12 inches) high. Therefore, if you have limited space and prefer the look of the lower pitchers, then keep your plant trimmed to a height of about 60cm (2 feet).

A typical form of the Nepenthes is one with a thick stem, of about 10 to 25mm (½ to 1 inch), connected to which are leaves which grow to about 45cm (18 inches). On the end of these leaves are the jug-like pitchers. Nepenthes often cling to other jungle trees and start to climb their way up, twisting around the trees to a height of up to 15 metres (50 feet) into the jungle canopies.

When growing wild the leaves are quite thick and tough, as is the tendril that attaches the pitcher to the leaf. As can be imagined, the pitchers themselves are quite heavy when half filled with insects and water, and feel quite firm to the touch. In comparison, hot house grown Nepenthes have much thinner and softer leaves and pitchers.

Species

NEPENTHES MIRABILIS

Nepenthes Mirabilis is one of the most common species, and is native to Borneo, New Guinea and Australia.

Pitchers on this plant are usually green and up to about 20 cm (8 inches) long, with tinges of red as the plant is exposed to increased sunlight. The leaves also take on this reddish tinge when exposed. The pitchers are usually cylindrical, often with a slight swelling towards the base, although this isn't always the case. Often the inside of the lid will be bright red, in stark contrast to the green pitchers. The wings, so prominent in many other varieties, notably Rafflesiana, are small if not absent altogether in Mirabilis.

There is such a variety from plant to plant in the Mirabilis in terms of both shape and colour that in times past the plant has been given other names, such as Rowanae, Alicae and Albo-Lineata, and as a result the description given above is only very general.

Nepenthes Mirabilis is one of the hardiest of all the Nepenthes and has the ability to withstand extreme heat, dryness and cool temperatures. However, best results are obtained if the plant is grown in a temperature range of between 15 and 30 degrees C. (60–85 degrees F.).

NEPENTHES AMPULLARIA

Found in Malaysia, Singapore, Sumatra, Borneo and New Guinea, the *Ampullaria* is known for its short, fat pitchers, which are generally 10 cm (4 inches) across, and coloured with red spots on a cream background. These pitchers usually sit on the ground. While most other species have a lid that prevents rain from flooding the pitchers, this plant has a lid that seems only to be effective when the plant has juvenile pitchers. As the pitcher matures the lid gradually falls back and then appears to serve no function.

The pitchers of the Ampullaria form from a short tendril around a rosette which develops from the stem. This rosette may have five or more pitchers, each with quite prominent wings. The stem itself seems to run along the ground to be buried by leaves and humus. About every 45 cm (18 inches) a new rosette of pitchers develops, which eventually develops its own root system, leaving the new rosette of pitchers independent of the original stem.

Nepenthes Ventricosa with juvenile pitchers in background

Nepenthes Alata with two unopened pitchers in back- ▼ ground

From each rosette the plant may also climb upwards to a height of up to nine metres (30 feet), developing rosettes and pitchers along the way. It is a strange sight to see a rosette of pitchers growing in what seems to be mid air, nine metres above the ground. The pitchers at this height differ from the lower ground pitchers, in that the former are longer, less fat, and usually greener.

NEPENTHES ALATA

Found in the Philippines and Malaysia, this plant has pitchers like a slender column. Towards the base the pitcher swells out. The pitcher grows to 12 cm (5 inches) long and usually has fringed wings. Given ample sunlight these pitchers turn a deep red.

This Nepenthes, like the Mirabilis, has variety within itself, with some pitchers being quite bulbous and others very slender. The upper pitchers are usually longer and more slender than the lower ones. The higher pitchers are also lacking in wings.

NEPENTHES ALBO-MARGINATA

The *Albo-Marginata* is found in Borneo, Malaysia and Sumatra in the swampy areas, in peat and sandy soil. As the name implies this plant has pitchers with a white band around the rim of the light green to reddish green pitchers. This lowland species can also have pitchers that are almost all red, although usually the base of the pitcher is a paler green to light tan colour.

The pitchers have prominent fringed wings and a lid matching the green or red of the pitcher. This is a very attractive plant with its "minister's collar" pitchers contrasting with the red or green rim. The pitchers usually are no bigger than 22 cm (9 inches).

Lower pitcher of Nepenthes Fusca ▼

NEPENTHES FUSCA

Found only in Borneo, the *Fusca* is a highland species which has very long, slender pitchers of 15 cm (6 inches) long and 3 cm (one inch) wide, and with what appears to be streaks of burgundy to red colour running down the length of the pitcher. There are so many streaks of colour that even though the pitchers have a green background, they appear a brown to black colour, as do the fringed wings and lid.

As this plant gets taller the pitchers become fatter and shorter; a characteristic quite the opposite to those of the upper pitchers of many Nepenthes species. It follows the general feature of having no wings on its upper pitchers.

Nepenthes Fusca grows on rock banks in clay soil areas that appear quite dry. The leaves on the plants in these areas are tough and rubbery, often taking on a burnt brown appearance as the older leaves absorb increased sunlight.

NEPENTHES GRACILIS

Borneo, Sumatra, Malaysia and Celebes are the native areas of the *Gracilis*. This plant has quite a few pitchers; although these are only 5 cm (2 inches) long the plant is prolific, and there may be five or more on a plant no bigger than 30 cm (12 inches) high.

Older pitchers of Gracilis are cylindrical and reddish pink in colour, as are the fringed wings, lid and inner part of the pitcher. Leaves of this plant are thin, only 1 to 3 cm (½ to 1 inch) and long: 20 cm (8 inches). These features, together with the fact that the stem is only 5 mm (¼ inch) wide, give the Gracilis an appearance of a very stringy, woody plant, with many pitchers for its size, and therefore ideally suited to the dry sandy ground the plant is found in.

Nepenthes
▼ *Gracilis*

NEPENTHES RAJAH

Borneo has about thirty of the total seventy species of Nepenthes. *Nepenthes Rajah* is by far the most impressive of the list, in terms of its shape, size and colour. Many believe this is the largest Nepenthes; however Nepenthes Merrilliana from the Philippines and Celebes, with its dark burgundy to almost black pitcher, rival the Rajah for size.

Nepenthes Rajah has pitchers which grow to 35cm (14 inches) long and are red to purple in colour. The lower pitchers are quite fat and bulbous, with fringed wings in the front. The upper pitchers are less winged and are tapered towards the tendril. The tendril doesn't begin from the tip of the leaf, rather from about 2.5 cm (one inch) below the tip.

Nepenthes Rajah, lower pitcher. Note where the tendril joins the leaf.

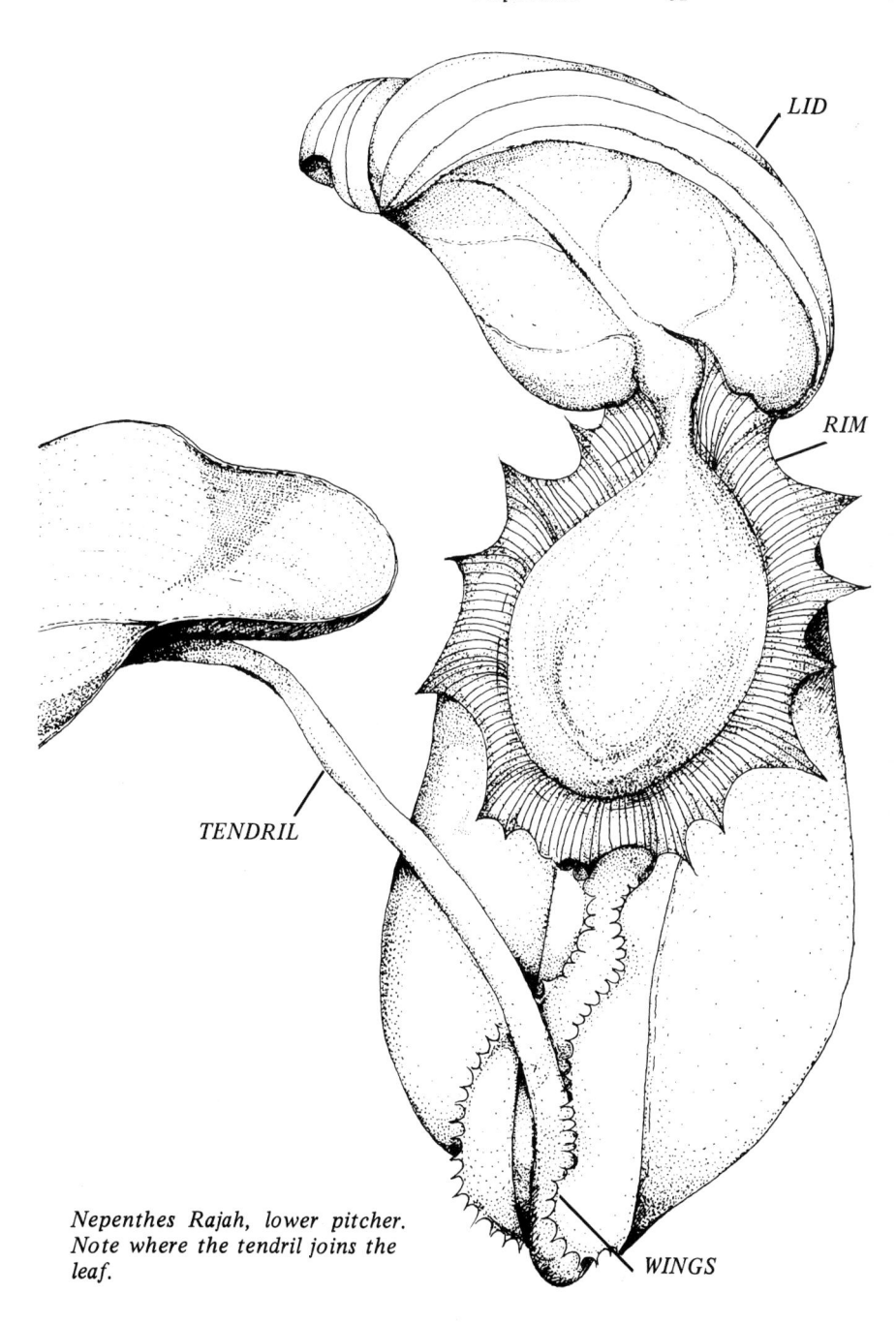

The leaves are very broad, being 15 cm (6 inches) wide.

This plant is a highland species which often grows around swamps and water falls, in ultrabasic, very wet soil. Ultrabasic is a type of soil that is almost clay-like; it contains less than 45% Silica, and is high in iron-magnesium silicate, which gives it its red colour.

The Rajah is very scarce in cultivation, but is certainly worth obtaining for its 50–80 cm (2–3 feet) flower stem; dark green 20–45 cm (8 to 18 inches) long leaves; and its huge pitchers, the size of footballs and purplish colour. All in all it makes for a very attractive hot house plant.

NEPENTHES RAFFLESIANA

The *Rafflesiana* is quite a common Nepenthes, found in Borneo, Malaysia, New Guinea, Singapore and Sumatra. It has light green to beige coloured pitchers with red to burgundy patches. The fronts of the pitchers have large wings that often curl inwards. The ribs on the rim are quite fine and very sharp. As this plant grows taller the shorter, fatter pitchers become thin and longer. While both the lid and the rim retain their colour the pitcher may lose its reddish appearance to turn a light green. One interesting point to note about the rim of the upper pitchers is that instead of being rounded, the front turns upwards, as if it has been pushed up. The upper pitchers can occur on this plant when it has reached a height of less than four feet (120 cm). The plant then continues to grow to reach the jungle canopy.

NEPENTHES SANGUINEA

The *Sanguinea* is a highland species found in Malaysia with pitchers often up to 30 cm (12 inches) long. These pitchers are cylindrical at the top, and become slightly swollen in shape at the base, 7 cm (3 inches) in diameter. While the photo shows the pitchers to be green they may also be deep crimson in some varieties. Its dark green leaves grow to 35 cm (14 inches) long and 12 cm (5 inches) wide.

CARE

Many glass houses grow tropical plants in the temperature range of 19 degrees C. and 25 degrees C. (65 to 77 degrees F.). This is the ideal temperature condition for the Nepenthes. The tempera-

Nepenthes Sanguinea: note the immature pitcher to the far right, lower pitcher middle, upper pitcher far left

ture range can be extended however, to between 15 degrees C. and 30 degrees C. (60 to 85 F.) and the plants will still do quite well. What is important is that the humidity should be at least 70% for most of the time, and ideally 90%.

With this degree of moisture-laden air the plant will develop large pitchers, and grow quite rapidly, with large plants often lengthening by three or more feet each year.

REPRODUCTION

While seed germination of Nepenthes is not difficult, it requires two plants, one male and one female, to be cross pollinated for the seeds to be viable. Unfortunately it isn't possible to know whether the plant is male or female until it flowers. Once it does identification is easy as only the flower of the male plant has stamen. The female plant receives pollen from the male on its stigma and seed is later produced in the ovary, as seen in the diagram.

Seeds should be placed in a clear, sealed plastic or glass container, in order to keep high humidity, avoid draughts and promote an even temperature.

While different Nepenthes require different growing conditions, as a general guide seeds should be given a bottom heat of about 19 degrees C. (65 F.); the ideal is 25 degrees C. (77 F.). Bottom heat simply means heating cables in the soil, providing a constant warm temperature. Planting seeds in live sphagnum moss has the advantage that the moss can be used as an indicator towards the right conditions. That is to say, the moss will stay green and lush when both light and humidity are right. There is however one disadvantage to using sphagnum. The moss will quickly grow and soon overtake any seedlings that might arise. This can be prevented by trimming with a pair of scissors.

Cuttings should be handled in the same way as seeds; the only difference being that they respond to having the stem dipped in a rooting hormone, such as "Rootine" or "Strike".

With a cutting, a section of the stem is either partly cut and then wrapped with sphagnum moss and held to the plant with plastic until roots begin to appear; the other method is to cut the stem fully and place it in sphagnum or peat moss with each section having one leaf. It is necessary to cut off and remove the section containing the pitchers from the cutting to be propogated. It is advisable to spray the cutting with fungicide (such as Benlate) before placing the cutting in either a heating misting bed or some sort of heated, high humidity container. Roots on a

STAMEN

Top left: male flower of Nepenthes
Lower left: female flower of Nepenthes ▲

Nepenthes: Seed pods ripening towards the base. ▶

cutting generally form after about one month, depending on the size of the cutting. After about two to three months the rooted cutting can be potted up.

A small hot house situated in a cool climate can be heated quite cheaply with a bit of ingenuity. What is required is to set up a small flow-through hot water service that warms the air. As warm water is used, the mist jets or foggers should be placed in the ground, having their spray directed upwards. Upon turning the tap on a small amount of water passing over the heating element will be warmed. This then flows through the mist jets, warms the air and thus increases humidity.

The whole system should be regulated by a solinoid valve, which in turn is controlled by a time clock. The frequency and length of time the system sprays for depends on the outside temperature and the glass house material. Be careful about hot water hitting the plants, which is why I suggest the foggers be placed on the ground.

If you cannot sustain temperatures of about 15 degrees C. (60 F.) at night and about 25 degrees C. (77 F.) during the day, then consider growing Nepenthes Khasiana. This plant is native to the highlands of India and can withstand quite cold temperatures, down to zero degrees C. (32 F.) during the night, and cool conditions, such as 10 degrees C. (50 F.), during the day.

Nepenthes can however be grown quite successfully without a glass house, in a glass terrarium. An old fish tank is ideal. To do this simply insert a shelf of a few inches above the bottom of the tank. On this shelf can be placed the Nepenthes pots. Now fill the tank with water until it is just below the shelf. In the water place an aquarium water heater, put a lid on the tank, and you will be surprised how quickly the temperature and humidity will rise. However, you must ensure that the Nepenthes do not touch the water underneath, as it can cause the roots to rot. This set-up can also be used to bring on seeds and seedlings.

9

Butterworts (Pinguiculas)

Pinguicula, or Butterwort, as it is more commonly known, derives its name from the fact that the leaves look fat and greasy. These leaves release a digestive liquid and acid which proceeds to dissolve the insect, as the leaf rolls up to engulf it.

One of the most appealing characteristics of the Pinguicula is the flower the plant produces. The colours include white, purple, mauve and yellow, and the flowers are quite large for such a small plant.

Many of the 48 known species come from Mexico and South America. The size of the plant varies from a minimum of 2.5 cm (1 inch) to a maximum of 20 cm (8 inches).

Distribution of Pinguiculas ▼

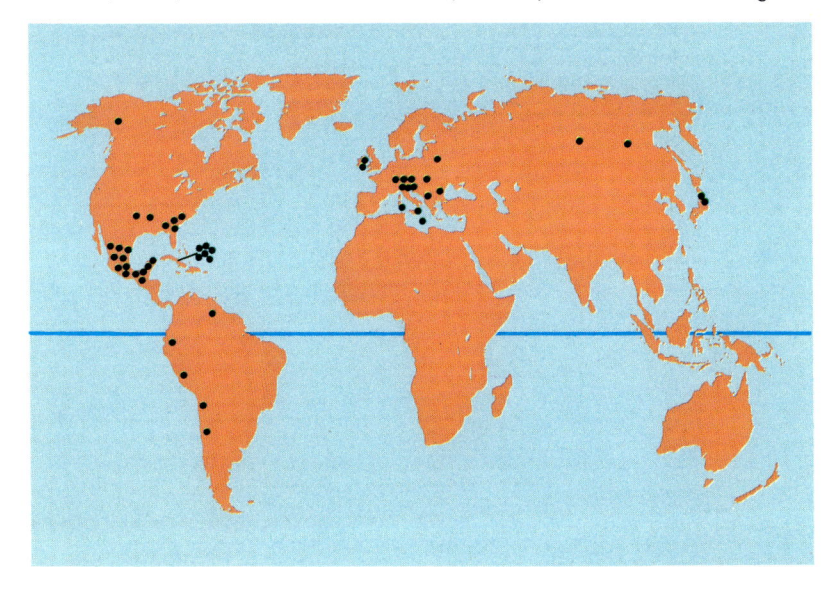

Pinguicula
▲ *Primuliflora*

Species

PINGUICULA PRIMULIFLORA

Found in shaded areas of North America, the *Primuliflora* has leaves of up to 10 cm (4 inches) across. The leaves are light green, and its flowers are violet. Like many Pinguiculas, new plants often establish themselves on the tips of the parent plant's leaves. In time these new plantlets form roots and can be potted up, and like the parent plant should be given filtered light.

PINGUICULA CAERULEA

Also from North America, the *Caerulea* looks like a star with its very pointed leaves. This plant also has deep violet to almost blue flowers. Its light green leaves are 6 cm (2½ inches) long and radiate out from the centre.

PINGUICULA CAUDATA

The *Caudata* is from Mexico and has fat, rounded leaves of up to 10 cm (4 inches) long, and very beautiful 5 cm (2 inch) wide purple flowers, appearing in both summer and winter on 15 to 22 cm (6–9 inch) stalks.

PINGUICULA LUTEA

Again from North America, the plant likes a little more sunlight than the Primuliflora, although they may grow well next to each other. *Lutea* has a large 2.5 cm (1 inch) wide, bright yellow flower, on a stem up to 30 cm (12 inches) high. Its leaves are shorter and broader than the Primuliflora. The Lutea grows best above a minimum temperature of 10 degrees C. (50 F.).

CARE

Pinguiculas can be grown in straight sphagnum moss, and watered from a tray. Stand the pot in a dish of water 10 to 20 mm deep (½ to 1 inch). Wait until the tray is dry, then top it up again to the previous level.

I have grown this genus quite successfully in peat moss and also in a mix of vermiculite and peat moss; this latter mixture appears especially good for plantlets.

While plantlets on the tips of leaves are quite a successful way of reproduction, the plant can also be grown from seed and leaf cuttings. As with most leaf cuttings, remove the leaf, including the white section of the base. Place this in moist sphagnum moss covered with a plastic bag, and give ample light. If you have used healthy winter leaves then plantlets should start appearing from the base of the leaf in about four to seven weeks after the first few leaves begin to appear. Keep this new plant fairly well protected for the next few months.

If the plantlets take longer than seven weeks to come I usually don't repot the seedling until the following winter. Pinguiculas don't like their roots disturbed too much, especially during summer.

Whether a plastic bag or terrarium is used for this cutting, ensure that droplets of water do not land on the plant by supporting the centre of the bag, or sloping the roof of the terrarium.

Pinguicula Gypsicola prior to dormancy

Inset: Pinguicula Gypsicola ▲ *in dormancy*

Many of the Pinguiculas grow well under grow-lux tubes or globes. This means having the light source about 30–40 cm (12–16 inches) above the plant, on a photo period of 14 hours in summer and 10 hours in winter. Then the temperature range is 25 degrees C. (77 F.) maximum in summer and 10 degrees C. (50 F.) in winter.

10

Bladderworts (*Utricularia*)

Although the *Utricularia* is very small its method of catching insects is by far the most ingenious of all the Carnivorous Plants. It is the largest genus of all the Carnivores with about 200 species, and as can be seen from the map, it is quite widespread. The exact figure is unknown as research in some regions is still incomplete.

Even though Charles Darwin named the Venus Fly Trap as the most wonderful plant in the world it was a toss up between that plant and the Utricularia. Perhaps its size let it down, or the fact that it was considered to have a simple trapping mechanism. However, recent evidence has proved that the trap is quite comp-

Distribution of Utricularia ▼

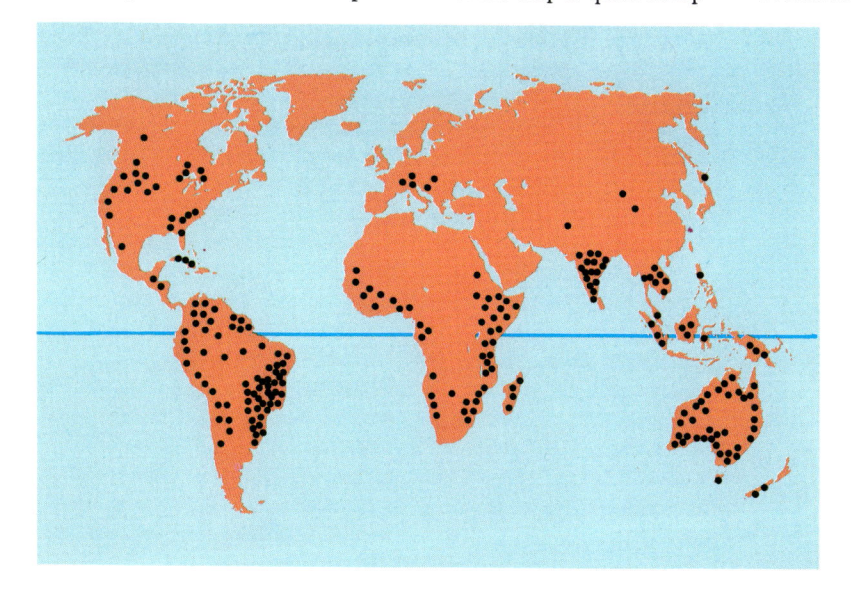

Utricularia

licated, and one wonders if in the light of this Darwin would have reconsidered his verdict.

As its more common name of Bladderwort implies, the Utricularia has bladders or small bubbles about the size of a match head which trap insects. These plants are either terrestrial, that is, they grow in soil; or acquatic, which means they exist submerged in water. They often have a main stem, and off this are branches, attached to which are the bladders.

Each of the bladders has tiny trigger hairs at the entrance. These are touched by passing prey, which springs the door to the bladder inwards, and the prey plus some water is sucked in. Quickly the door shuts and the prey is captured. The excess water then leaves the bladder, until the plant returns to its original vacuum state ready to be triggered again.

Species
UTRICULARIA CALYCIFIDA

Utricularia
▼ *Calycifida*

This plant is native to Venezuala, and is terrestrial, with large light green leaves 12 to 19 mm (½ to ¾ inch) wide and 12 to 25 mm (½ to 1 inch) long. Under ideal conditions of reduced light and a warm greenhouse the leaves of this plant can grow to 10 cm (4 inches). *Calycifida* is best planted in live sphagnum moss, and left sitting in a tray of water.

UTRICULARIA PYGMAEA

Native to Australia, the *Utricularia Pygmaea* is one of the terrestrial species with very small 2 mm flowers of a yellow to white colour. The leaves of this plant form at the base of the stem and are at most 1 cm long, and light green in colour. The Pygmaea is a very prolific plant ideally suited to terrariums.

Utricularia floating in water with small bladders appearing as translucent bubbles ◀

UTRICULARIA AUSTRALIS

Also called Negelecta, this plant is widely spread throughout the tropics, common to Australia, New Zealand, South Africa and Japan. *Australis* is aquatic and like the Pygmaea very prolific. Being acquatic means that the plant floats on the surface of the water. Like the above two Utricularia this plant has small bladders, but is different in having no leaves. Australis has a large yellow flower rising to 7 cm (3 inches) above the water level.

Aquatic Utricularis need to be grown in a fish tank, bucket or some other sort of water holding container. To set this container up, moisten peat moss with rain water, and place this moist peat moss in a container to about 5 cm (2 inches). Now fill the container with rain water until the level is 10 cm (4 inches) above the moss. After about one week the moss will settle on the bottom of the container, and the water will begin to clear. It is

Utricularia bladders ready for prey

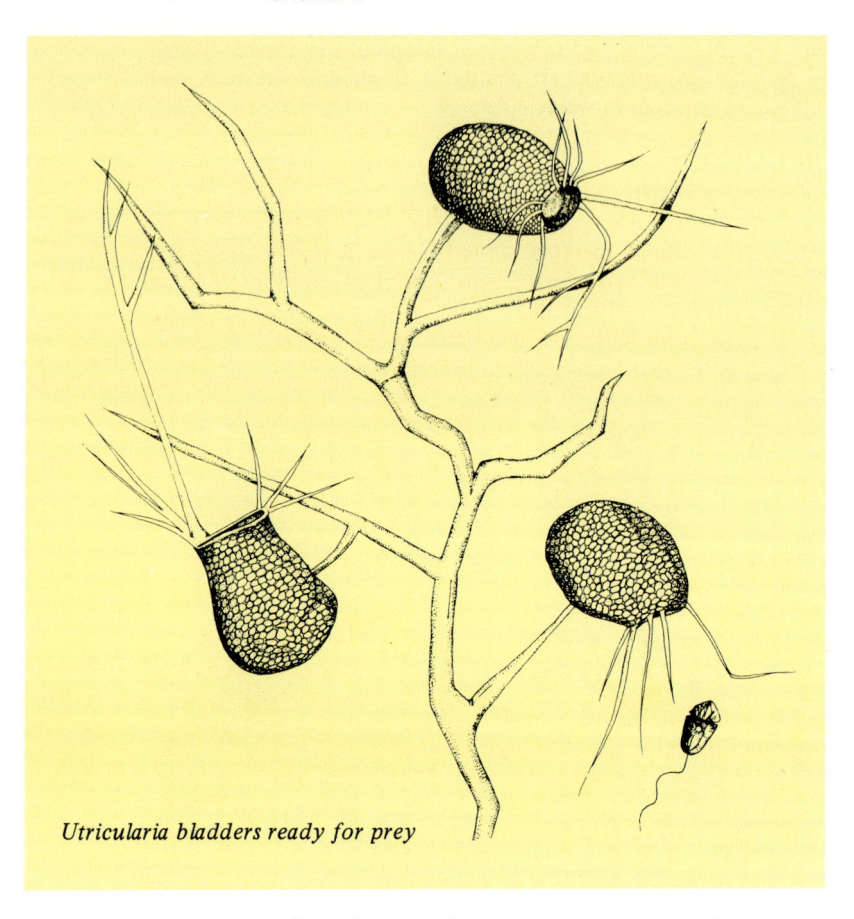

now time to place the Utricularia on the surface, and all that you need do is keep the water topped up.

Remember to use rainwater, and add it over time instead of great amounts at once.

UTRICULARIA MENZIESII

Menziesii is native to West Australia and is found in very wet soil. This plant has bright red to burgundy coloured flowers, about one cm (3/8 inch) long and bright green leaves up to 7 mm (¼ inch) long.

An interesting feature of this Utricularia is that it has a resting corm to help the plant survive through the dry summer. This corm is similar to a bulb in that it has storage tissue pro-

Utricularia Menziesii with flower ◄

tected by an outer leaf covering. Unlike other Carnivorous Plants this plant has a summer dormancy and should be allowed to dry out over this time. The plant will come back as water is increased over the winter period to flower early with renewed vigor. I pot this plant into a soil mix of two parts sphagnum moss, one part peat moss and one part vermiculite, and keep it well watered. This is a plant well worth adding to your collection; its attractive flower appearing at a time when most of the other Carnivorous Plants are in winter dormancy.

11

Cobra Lily
(Darlingtonia Californica)

Darlingtonia like the Cephalotus has only one member of its genus. It is native to California and Oregon in the USA. This plant grows to a maximum height of one metre (39 inches) and has a similar trapping mechanism to that of Sarracenias.

This plant is commonly called a Cobra Lily as its tall pitchers have a large hood and fangs resembling those of the cobra snake. It is these fangs which turn red to burgundy and flare out from the pitcher that make this plant look so impressive.

The pitchers of the Darlingtonia have downward pointing hairs on the inside similar to that of the Sarracenia species. The mirror maze type trap makes the Cobra Lily similar to the Sarra-

Distribution of Darlingtonia Carlifornica ▼

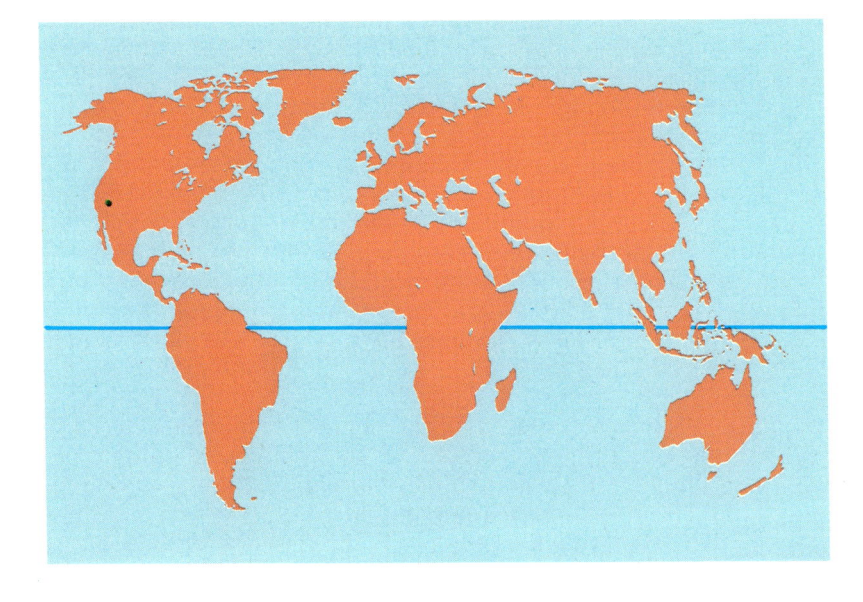

cenia Psittacina in particular. Insects are attracted to the plant by its colour and scent. On the fangs just inside the pitcher rim nectar is secreted to lure the insect down into the pitcher. Clear patches on the hood cause windows of light to confuse the insect once it has crawled inside. The buzzing of a trapped insect is often heard around the hood as the insect attempts to escape via these windows of light, all to no avail. In time the prey makes its way down to the base of the plant to be decomposed by bacterial action.

Initially the Darlingtonia begins to grow with juvenile leaves, which radiate from the centre of the plant. From the centre mature leaves suddenly begin to appear. As can be seen from the photograph opposite, these leaves are quite different from the juvenile leaves in that they have small fangs and a flat hood. As the pitcher grows the fangs become bigger and the hood puffs out. As the first pitcher is growing to maturity others start to appear. All will grow to about the same height as the first, except for one pitcher which will keep growing, exceeding the height of those surrounding it. A new lot of pitchers will grow to this new height, and the cycle starts again. This is how the plant develops an appearance similar to that of a pyramid.

An interesting characteristic of this plant is that the pitchers begin by facing the centre of the plant, then start twisting, until they eventually face away from the centre. This twisting is accompanied by a decrease in height.

It is exciting to watch a pitcher grow very straight and tall, then see it gradually twisting to join the height of its brothers. Upon seeing the new pitchers emerge you never know whether a new pitcher will grow to the present height or be the leader of a new group.

Spring sees the emergence of the purplish to almost red flowers which rise on stems above the pitchers. Like the Sarracenia one flower appears on each stem, dangling downwards. Seeds can be collected from these flowers and should be stored in the refrigerator for a few months. This will simulate the plant's native winter period. After three to five months the seeds can be planted on peat or sphagnum moss, covered with plastic and left until seedlings appear.

Another method of reproduction is to remove the new plantlets that grow on the ends of the rhyzome. In large containers the rhyzome in the Darlingtonia runs to the edge of the pot and sends up new pitchers; these in time develop roots and can be treated like new plants. Like that of the Cephalotus

Darlingtonia Californica

Cobra Lily: the older pitchers have red fangs

Inset: Juvenile leaves ▲

Follicularis this rhyzome can be cut into 2.5 cm (1 inch) sections and planted in peat moss. Ensure there is ample spacing between the cuttings to avoid crowding, otherwise the young seedlings will experience a root disturbance. If moved too soon the roots may break and the seedling subsequently die.

As with most Carnivorous Plants rain water should be used, and humidity kept high. Ensure the plant experiences a winter dormancy of three months and isn't subjected to excessive heat. Watch the fangs of the young pitchers for signs of ill health; on days of extreme heat they will begin to curl up and go brown. This can also happen if excessive heat is experienced in a terrarium.

CARE

Darlingtonia is certainly an interesting plant and worthwhile adding to your collection; however the plant must have a cool root system, otherwise the purplish coloured flowers will not appear in the late spring to early summer period as they should. A cool root system can be obtained by growing the plant in large concrete tubs filled with sphagnum moss. If you need to grow the plant in a hot house then consider using polystyrene boxes. These keep the roots at an even temperature. An even more effective system can be achieved by having cool water pass through the box with the aid of a small electric motor. While this may seem a bit elaborate, in its natural habitat the plant experiences hot days yet still has a cool root· system, growing as it does near streams and swamps.

Rainbow Plant (Byblis)

*T*his genus has two species, the *Gigantea* and the *Liniflora*, and both are native to Australia. While these plants are large compared to the Drosera, stories of them catching rabbits and similar sized prey are quite untrue. They are often mistaken for Drosera but there are major differences between *Byblis* and Drosera. The first is that the Byblis are passive plants; unlike the Drosera which has tentacles that move to capture the prey, the Byblis has sticky hairs that don't move. The other difference which is in the plant's flower structure causes the two Byblis to be placed in their own genus, separate from Drosera.

Distribution of Byblis ▼

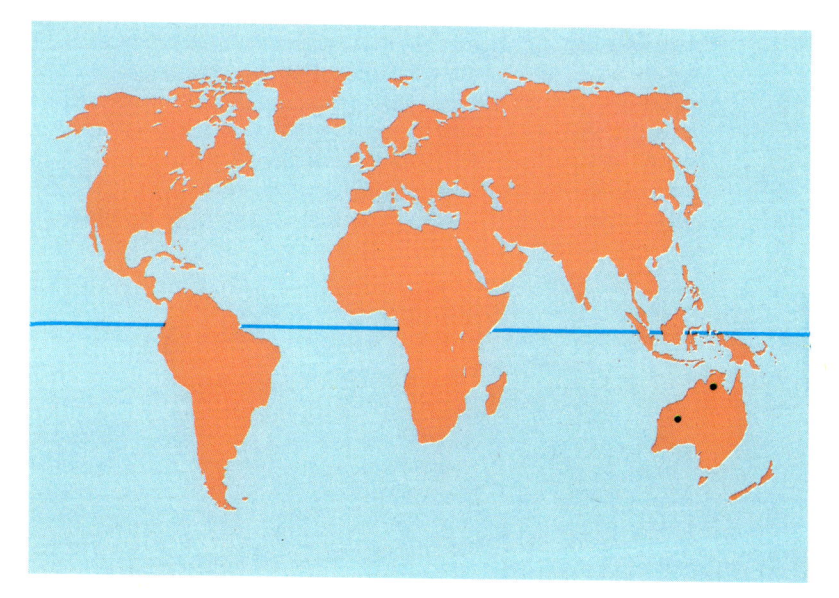

Species

BYBLIS GIGANTEA

This Byblis is only found in West Australia. It stands erect and is a very tall plant, growing up to 60 cm (2 feet) high. The *Gigantea* is a very prolific flowerer with often five or more purple or lilac flowers appearing at any one time. Flowers usually appear in the spring, and have petals of 2 cm (¾ inch) long.

This plant exists in sandy swamps and dies back each summer with the emergence of hot weather. The plant will then stay dormant until winter rains begin. However in cultivation the plant may not go into dormancy.

The Gigantea has a very woody stem and the plant may be cut back to this after a couple of years if it starts to become too stringy. Pot the plant into a soil mix of half peat and half sand. Allow adequate drainage and do not stand in water. Then like the Sarracenia it will return with increased vigour the following season.

Byblis
▲ *Gigantea*

BYBLIS LINIFLORA

Liniflora is more widespread in Australia than the Gigantea and is found in the Northern Territory and Queensland as well as West Australia. Not as rigid as the Gigantea, the Liniflora is often straggly with such a weak root system that the plant is often forced to lie along the ground. Like the Gigantea the Liniflora has several flowers on the one stem which are a blue-pink colour with petals 1 cm (½ inch) long. The flowers appear during the wet season from December to April.

Liniflora flourishes near water courses, usually in shaded areas, and grows up to 30 cm (12 inches) tall. When growing this plant use a soil mix of half peat and half sand, keep moist and in a fairly warm position.

Summer Growth & Winter Dormancy

SUMMER GROWTH

*I*f your plant has been sitting in soil over the winter period, and if tap water was used, then it may be necessary to change the soil to prevent any build-up of salts, etc. Once the plant has been re-potted, the pot can then be placed in a tray of water about 12mm to 25mm (½ to 1 inch). However, a tray of water should not be used for Nepenthes, Butterworts and some Drosera.

Generally, if the leaves are tall and stringy, then this is usually due to lack of light, and possible lack of water.

As a guide to a plant in good condition:

Venus Fly Traps develop red traps as summer approaches.

Albany Pitcher Plant will develop a red tinge around the rim of the pitcher, and on the lid. If humidity is low the lid will close. Flower stem(s) will begin to grow on mature plants, to about 18 inches, and have small white petals.

New leaves will appear on Sarracenias in spring, and flowers on mature plants about late spring, depending on the species, and the degree of dormancy the plant experienced over winter.

Nepenthes should have both healthy green leaves and pitchers with open lids. Once again the pitchers will often go red or have red spots, depending on the species.

A sick looking plant as a rule should have its dead leaves and pitchers cut off.

Albany Pitcher Plants can sometimes die back if repotted, but provided the root system is large enough, the plant will soon adjust and start sending up new pitchers and leaves. If the lid on the pitcher closes and the pitcher begins to go soft, then cover the plant with plastic and protect from sunlight, until the plant picks up again.

Droseras will usually go dry with no droplets of water on the tentacles if the humidity or water is decreased. Covering the plant with a plastic bag should solve the problem, until the plant is moved to a better location with higher humidity. A fungus could occur on this plant if in a terrarium, or where air circulation is poor, in which case, spray with Benlate.

Pinguiculas or Butterworts will usually go brown and rot if the plant is sitting in water, as will Nepenthes. If kept in terraria, these plants should be arranged so that their roots are not constantly wet. Often Nepenthes will not form pitchers if the roots are wet or the humidity is low.

WINTER DORMANCY

Generally decrease the amount of overhead watering; and if the plant is sitting in a tray of water, then decrease that water level too.

In our hot houses, no plants, except Utricularia, are sitting in water during the winter period. As a precaution trim off the dead leaves and spray all plants with Benlate at the start of Winter. This should decrease the chance of fungus destroying your collection. Many growers spray again in mid-Winter and re-trim off all dead leaves.

Venus Fly Traps can be taken out of the soil, all leaves trimmed off and the bulb placed in a refrigerator (not freezer) until the emergence of Spring.

If you have used shadecloth to decrease sunlight over Summer this may be removed, especially for growers living in cooler areas.

Most Carnivorous Plants can withstand quite cold conditions; an exception to this is the Nepenthes. These should be kept in warm conditions, at least above 10 degrees C. (50 F.)

Don't be too worried about the tops of leaves browning off or going black. (With the Sarracenia Oreophylla all the pitchers of older plants will usually disappear). The plant will be all right, provided the bulb does not rot due to over-watering.

If you have your plants in a terrarium then leave the lid off and allow the soil to dry out a little; close the lid and leave it alone until Spring. If you are using grow-lux tubes then decrease the number of hours the light is left on. The photo period does depend on the position and type of plants, but as a general rule about half to two-thirds of the photo period in summer time, or eight to twelve hours.

14

Peat Gardens & Terraria

SETTING UP A CARNIVOROUS PEAT GARDEN.

*I*t is difficult to suggest conditions suitable for every type of area, as different plants are affected by different temperatures and rainfall. The position of the peat garden should be one that has some filtered light, similar to that for ferns and orchids.

Set up a peat garden for carnivorous plants by digging a

Peat
▶*Garden*

hole at least 60 cm deep, (2 feet), but preferably up to 120 cm (4 feet). The deeper one goes, the less likely the garden will dry out. Line this with thick plastic then fill with damp peat moss, soaked for a few days beforehand. Water this well and let settle for a few more days. After the moss has settled your carnivores can be taken out of their pots and added directly to the peat.

Section of Peat Garden ▲

    We have successfuly grown Venus Fly Traps, Sarracenias, Utricularia, Cephalotus, some Drosera and Pinguicula Primuliflora in this type of garden. Of course such tropical plants as Nepenthes require a very warm temperature and may not grow in your area outdoors. As with a terrarium, a peat garden looks best with tall Sarracenias towards the back and the shorter plants such as Drosera, Venus Fly Trap, Cephalotus Follicularis and Utricularia towards the front, in that order. Once the plants have been added to the garden and watered well, green sphagnum moss can be placed around the plants as an insulator and also as an indicator that the peat is damp enough.
    Some plants may look a little poor at first but they will soon adjust to the conditions now similar to the swamps they are native to. An outside peat garden has the advantages that the plants are hardier, easier to look after and usually go through a better winter dormancy than those grown in the house or in a glass house.

    Once the garden is established, as well as being an insect free (or at least less insects than before) area to sit and enjoy, there will usually be at least one species in flower at any one time.

TERRARIA

A terrarium is simply a sealed container that provides a moisture-balanced environment. So balanced is this environment that terraria, or "Wardian Cases" as they were known in the 1800's, were used to transport plants across the world. Often the cases were sealed for months and even years, with the plants thriving in their own balanced eco-system.

Terraria can be used for growing most carnivorous plants, and they can be made of either glass or plastic.

The advantage of terraria is that they contain the heat to a large extent and provide a more even range of temperature, while keeping a high humidity level and protecting the plants

Flat roofed terrarium with Venus Fly Trap, Drosera Hamiltoni and Cephalotus Follicularis in foreground: Sarracenias as a backdrop

from draughts. Terraria make it possible to have healthy plants indoors in atmospheres that might otherwise be dry, causing the plants to dry out and eventually die. Terraria also provide the focal point for an attractive arrangement of plants.

However they do have disadvantages: excessive heat can build up very quickly when they are left in direct sunlight, and there is a greater chance of disease developing on the plant once it has entered the terrarium.

To prevent the plants from overheating, place the terrarium in a room with ample light but away from direct sunlight, especially when the sun is at its maximum intensity. To prevent disease, spray the terrarium with Benlate as soon as it is planted up.

There are many different types of soil mixes that can be used in terraria. Most satisfactory is three parts peat moss, one part sphagnum moss, one part vermiculite and one part sand; all together about three inches deep. However, straight peat moss or straight sphagnum is still quite a successful mix.

METHOD

Before you begin planting the Terrarium group the plants in the arrangement you intend to use. Check the heights, ensuring that there are both tall and short plants; ensure there is a good mix of colour and that the Terrarium won't be overcrowded.

After much experimenting, I find the best method is to remove the plants from their pots, keeping some soil surrounding their roots, and place the whole into the terrarium soil. Start with the largest plant then continue planting until all the plants are in. The last to add is the sphagnum moss. Water this immediately, until the peat moss is quite damp. After doing this, you could seal the terrarium around the edges of the lid with tape, and never have to water it again, providing it has stabilized and created its own balanced environment, and is kept in the right position.

If after a few days you find that the terrarium doesn't fog up at all and the soil is a light tan colour, then add a little water day by day until the terrarium has fogged up a little and the soil has turned dark brown to almost black in colour. This then is a guide to a balanced system.

Terraria can be kept sealed for many years, as they create their own life support system, - of decay, nitrogen, oxygen and carbon dioxide.

For a carnivorous plant, insects are a bonus, similar to giving a plant a boost with a fertilizer; therefore the lack of insects will not do the plant any harm. If you really feel the need to fertilize your terrarium then do so in spring, using a liquid fertilizer at half the weakest strength. This fertilizer may be added using a hand sprayer; a couple of squirts is adequate. However, some of the best looking carnivorous plants are gown in sealed terraria, with no fertilizer.

While many individuals catch insects, throw them into the terrarium, then sit back and watch the show, I have never done this nor found the thought of it particularly entertaining.

If you want to give your plants extra care, then you could install grow lights above the terrarium, allowing for fifteen hours maximum in summer, and from eight to twelve hours in winter. This could be regulated by a timer: don't try to push your plants on by having lights on 24 hours a day. It is vital for plants to have their rest period.

One point worth mentioning is that a terrarium with a sloping roof will allow water droplets to run down the side of the terrarium, as is preferable, rather than land on top of the plant, as would happen with flat-roofed terraria.

When planting, if your terrarium has a mirror back, plant the tall plants, Sarracenias, at the back, with the smaller plants, for instance Venus Fly Traps and Cephalotus, towards the front. If the terrarium has no mirror back, then place the tall plants in the middle and the other smaller plants around them. Both these arrangements provide an interesting visual back-drop. You could also add other non-carnivorous plants such as Birds Nest Fern (Asplenium Nidus) or Asparagus Fern (Asparagus Plumosus) as well as pine cones, rocks, branches etc. In fact for larger terraria the area can be contoured with hills and valleys; this together with fallen leaves can result in a natural looking woodland scene.

Green sphagnum moss is a good ground cover over the peat mix; it helps to control the water level, while providing a little extra colour. However, in such humid conditions the sphagnum moss can grow very rapidly, and requires regular trimming with small scissors. Thus it is not really suitable for terraria that will be sealed for a long time.

If you don't have a green thumb, or you don't have any land to grow Carnivorous Plants, or you feel indoors may get too dry for your plants, then terraria are the safest way to grow your

Mirror back terrarium with tall plants towards the back, rocks and sphagnum moss in foreground

carnivorous plants; also one of the best ways to bring up seeds, look after sick plants and strike most cuttings. The species suitable for terraria include Sarracenias, Venus Fly Trap, Cephalotus, Drosera, some Pinguicula, and also Nepenthes, if given adequate drainage.

However don't forget this natural "perfect" environment is also ideal for diseases, so keep a sharp lookout for any sign of ill health, and quickly remove any decaying leaves or flowers. If necessary remove the decaying plant until all such decay has stopped. When the plant looks healthy again it can be returned to the terrarium. It may also be necessary to remove some soil from around the plant before replacing it.

Equipment Required

1. Rainwater container
2. Peat Moss
3. Sphagnum Moss
4. Vermiculite
5. Mini Max Thermometer
6. Benlate
7. Watering Trays
8. Hygrometer to measure humidity
9. Hand Sprayer
10. Two inch pots
11. Four inch pots
12. Plant labels
13. Gloves
14. Propagating box
15. Sharp knife for division
16. Glass tank for propagation or Utricularia
17. Strike rooting hormone

The above list is intended purely as a guide, and hence consists of only basic items required; many can be substituted for equipment you have at hand.

References

A. Slack, *Carnivorous Plants*. A.H. & A.W. Reed Pty Ltd., England, 1980.

R. Schwartz, *Carnivorous Plants*. Praeger Publishers, Inc., USA, 1974.

Carnivorous Plant Newsletter.

Katsuhiko Kondo & Masahiro Kondo, *Carnivorous Plants of the World in Colour*. Ienohikari Association, Tokyo, 1983.

D.E. Schnell, *Carnivorous Plants of the US and Canada*. Blaire, 1976.

Cassels Popular Gardening. Printed in 1800s.

A.B. Graf, *Exotica*. Roehrs Company, Inc., New Jersey.

Durland Fish, "Insect–Plant Relationships of the Insectivorous Pitcher Plant Sarracenia Minor", from *Florida Entomologist* Vol. 59, No. 2. Dept. of Entomology and Nematology, University of Florida, Gainesville.

Charles Darwin, *Insectivorous Plants*. Appleton Company, New York, 1892

Journal of the Elisha Mitchell Scientific Society, 1928, 1949, 1952, 1956.

J.M. MacFarlane, *Nepenthaceae*. Das Pflanzenreich, Leipzig, 1908.

S. Kurata, *Nepenthes of Mt. Kinabalu*. Sabah National Park, 1976.

Rica Erikson, *Plants of Prey in Australia*. Lamp Publishing, Australia, 1968.

F.E. Lloyd, *The Carnivorous Plants*. Dover Publications Inc., New York, 1976.

B.H. Danser, *The Nepenthaceae of the Netherlands Indies*. Bull. Jard. bot, Buit., Ser III Vol. IX 1928, Ser III Vol. XIII 1935.

J. & P. Pietropaolo, *The World of Carnivorous Plants*. R.J. Stoneridge, New York, 1974.

Scientific American, July 3, 1875, & December 18, 1909.